September

Day by Day
with
God

Rooting women's lives in the Bible

The Bible Reading Fellowship
15 The Chambers, Vineyard
Abingdon OX14 3FE
brf.org.uk

The Bible Reading Fellowship (BRF) is a Registered Charity (233280)

ISBN 978 0 85746 913 7

Distributed in Australia by:
MediaCom Education Inc, PO Box 610, Unley, SA 5061
Tel: 1 800 811 311 | admin@mediacom.org.au

Distributed in New Zealand by:
Scripture Union Wholesale, PO Box 760, Wellington
Tel: 04 385 0421 | suwholesale@clear.net.nz

Acknowledgements

Printed by Gutenberg Press, Tarxien, Malta

Day by Day with God

Edited by Jill Rattle
September–December 2020

Writers in this issue

Lakshmi Jeffreys is a wife, mother, sister, vicar, friend, dog-walker and school governor. Her booklet on singleness was published shortly after she met the man she eventually married.

Christine Platt is a writer and ESOL teacher. For the last 16 years she has ministered in East Timor, and she has written a book about her experiences – *Glimpses of God in Chaos*. She also teaches English to Asian students.

Michele D. Morrison is a passionate believer excited by what God is doing. A freelance writer, she loves listening for God's voice in the daily routines of life and blogging at **tearsamidthealiencorn.com** and on Facebook.

Lyndall Bywater is a freelance writer, trainer and consultant in all things prayer. She has a passion for helping people get to know God better, and is the author of two books for BRF: *Faith in the Making* and *Prayer in the Making*.

Diana Archer is an educator, writer and speaker with a theological background. She cofounded the charity **tastelifeuk.org**, which trains people to offer hope and tools for recovery to those with eating disorders and to their supporters.

Selina Stone is tutor and lecturer in Political Theology at St Mellitus College. She is also a part-time PhD student at the University of Birmingham, her home city, researching liberation and justice in Pentecostal theology and ministry.

Deborah Humphries is a minister in the Methodist Church in Birmingham and helped develop the Holy Habits resources for use there and for wider use. She is passionate about growing disciples and building community.

Helen Williams has worked in music, education, management consultancy and administration. She currently finds herself working alongside her husband, an Anglican bishop, in some fabulously diverse contexts, while continuing to work as an accompanist.

Karin Ling has a background in creative writing in the media. She served on the staff of Christ Church, Winchester, for four years before returning to freelance writing to fit around being a very busy mother of four.

Claire Musters is an author, speaker and editor. Her books include *Taking Off the Mask: Daring to be the person God created you to be*. Her blog covers issues about marriage, parenting, authenticity and discipleship. Visit **clairemusters. com** and **@CMusters** on Twitter.

Jill Rattle writes...

Recently Tom, a smiley and heavily tattooed forklift driver, joined our church and had a wonderful, life-transforming encounter with Jesus. He soon learned about prayer and started asking God for a full-time work contract to meet his financial needs. To his delight, he was called for interview. The interviewers worked through a number of mundane work-related questions with him and then finally one of them asked, 'So, Tom, what do you count as the greatest achievement of your life so far?' He thought and then answered: 'Well, about two months ago I became a Christian, and soon I'm going to be baptised; that's my greatest achievement.' He got the job!

How great is that! I wonder, in his place, would I have declared the same thing? It is so inspiring to watch Tom excitedly exploring his new faith.

Is there a danger for those of us who have been Christians for a long time to go a bit 'flat', to lose the joy and excitement of following Jesus? Could we even include ourselves in the criticism levelled by the Spirit to the church of Ephesus who were still faithful: 'But I have this against you, that you have abandoned the love you had at first' (Revelation 2:4, NRSV).

How do we maintain that 'first love', love that has matured but is still passionate for the things of God? Surely a big part of that is daily immersing ourselves in God's word with the expectation that we will encounter Jesus himself by the power of the Spirit – and every day have our love rekindled.

I worship in a church where someone left because they thought the leadership used the word 'excited' too much. As the vicar said, I think I'd rather be criticised for too much passion than too little! And it seems Jesus would agree with that – he wasn't keen on the 'lukewarm' (Revelation 3:16).

Our contributors in these notes are certainly not lukewarm. They are passionate about Jesus and the scriptures and feel privileged to share that love with you.

We welcome three new contributors in this issue: Deborah Humphries, a Methodist minister, explores the letter to the Colossians; Karen Ling, mother of four, writes about listening and learning from Jesus in our pressurised lives; and opening this edition with her notes on Book 5 of the Psalms is Lakshmi Jeffreys, an Anglican vicar.

Let's journey in faith together.

Prayerful imagination: Psalms Book 5

Lakshmi Jeffreys writes:

We live in an age of information overload, whether 24-hour news or constant feeds through social media: the reports of our family and friends' births, illnesses, jobs, marriages, etc. It is easy to feel overwhelmed and to struggle to distinguish what is important within the vast array of available material. In such circumstances, prayer can become another activity to be crammed into an already over-full day. The resulting feelings of duty or guilt can blind us to God's mercy, grace, love and acceptance.

The book of Psalms offers an antidote to this malaise. Perhaps more than other books in the Bible, it speaks to the emotions and allows the imagination to run free, going beyond what we see and hear. Imagination – the ability to form pictures in the mind or to have new ideas – helps us to manage information. Inspired, challenged, comforted or otherwise moved by a psalm, prayer becomes a natural response as we realign ourselves with the living God. The strong corporate side of the Psalms is a reminder that God calls us not in isolation but alongside all God's people: perspective returns.

The book of Psalms is sometimes called 'the hymn book of the Bible'. Using repetition and rhythm, psalms are designed to be recited or sung aloud – hence previous generations knew them by heart. Many hymns and worship songs include verses from the Psalms. I find it easier to remember words set to music and I discover psalms come to mind on various occasions.

When praying, I regularly employ words written by other people, whether composed hundreds of years ago for corporate church worship or by an individual for personal use. These prayers are seasonal, not in terms of spring or autumn but the seasons of life. I have a similar experience with the psalms: some are constant companions in prayer, while others reappear as lost friends at just the right time.

My dear friends reminded me recently of faithful Christian women whose busy lives do not permit lengthy periods of prayer or study, but also of the requirement to handle the Old Testament with integrity. As a result, I urge you, where possible, to take time slowly to read aloud the whole psalm of the day. Allow your imagination free rein, and your day will be punctuated with prayerful responses to God.

At the start

I will give thanks to you, O Lord, among the peoples, and I will sing praises to you among the nations. For your steadfast love is higher than the heavens. (NRSV)

What are you like as you face a day that will be filled with people you find challenging or who oppose your ideas? Do your thoughts, actions and feelings change according to the demands? Whatever your response to these questions, today's psalm is wonderful to read first thing in the morning or before you embark on difficult tasks ahead: it offers a pattern of prayer which can sustain you in the most taxing circumstances.

Jessica, a senior manager in her company, was on the committee of a local voluntary organisation. She was highly respected at work and well liked as a volunteer. Unfortunately Jessica's company was in conflict with the voluntary organisation. Jessica herself could see both sides of the argument but was jostled by each party to agree with their perspective. Despite this, she managed to remain calm and maintain confidences as individuals spoke to her. You might imagine her trepidation when a meeting arose in the voluntary organisation and some of the volunteers suggested a social media campaign against the company. Jessica felt as if she had been dragged into battle.

According to the pattern of the psalm, Jessica prayed during the meeting for all the people around her, praising God that God knew them and held them. (I find it interesting that Moab and the other nations opposed to God's people in the psalm were actually the countries that surrounded them – the enemy were their immediate neighbours!) She began to realise that this was not her fight, nor that of either group she represented. Instead God would grant victory: Jessica's task was to discover God's cause.

Our worries and concerns are real, and they can change with circumstances. Meanwhile, Jesus remains Lord of everyone and everything. We can praise him among friends and enemies and trust him.

God knows our allies and our enemies by name and has all things under control: how might this knowledge help you to pray in challenging circumstances?

LAKSHMI JEFFREYS

Praying for the enemy

In return for my love they accuse me, even while I make prayer for them. So they reward me evil for good, and hatred for my love… Help me, O Lord my God! Save me according to your steadfast love. (NRSV)

Many of us have faced bullying, prejudice or worse. Today's psalm expresses the agony David feels at the taunts of his enemies. In return, David initially asks God to bring to them all the misfortune they wanted to heap on David. Then he remembers his own relationship with God and begins to recognise God's care. The enemy might curse him, but God will bless him and will deliver the needy from those who would condemn them to death.

When I was a child, my parents, Indian immigrants, were the local GPs. A number of people knew the whereabouts not only of the surgery but also of our home. It was an era of political extremism and violence, and I have vivid memories, aged five years, of a brick being thrown through the sitting-room window early one evening, landing in my baby sister's playpen. Thankfully she was not in it; but I was petrified. Some years later we received a series of phone calls in the early hours of the morning. The caller would ascertain that my father was the doctor and would proceed to say that my father would die. My father would agree that yes, one day he would die, before he calmly replaced the phone. Despite my father's cool approach, as a young teenager I was terrified. Even today I encounter people who are (politely) hostile because of my ethnicity.

It is tempting to retaliate, but it is better to take time to reflect on God's love for us. Jesus knew rejection but has overcome all suffering and death. He walks with us through our trials. His Spirit teaches us how to overcome evil with good.

'If someone does you wrong, don't try to pay them back by hurting them. Try to do what everyone thinks is right. Do the best you can to live in peace with everyone' (Romans 12:17–18, ERV).

LAKSHMI JEFFREYS

Prayerful musical imagination

The Lord is my strength and my song; he has become my salvation.
(ESV)

Music has always been an important aspect of my life. Even people who claim to be unmoved by music engage in corporate singing. Watch a sporting event when a country's national anthem is played; go to a WI meeting when 'Jerusalem' strikes up; worship at any church with a competent music group or organist – and you will find the least musical individual is swept up in the proceedings. And woe betide the person who puts familiar words to an unfamiliar tune or sings a new setting of a favourite song!

In the introduction I mentioned that the psalms are designed to be said or sung aloud. Psalm 118 is especially suited to this, with refrains of 'His love endures forever' and a call-and-response feel in much of the psalm. Try reading it aloud yourself and hear how you chant the words. I find this makes a difference to how I subsequently encounter God. So often I imagine a man's voice, but what I think of when I read about battles and enemies differs completely from what my husband or son might think of. Similarly, the word 'strength' in scripture has more emotional and spiritual overtones than physical for me. And since the gender of the narrator is not specified, why not have a woman's song of thanksgiving?

The Magician's Nephew by C. S. Lewis tells the story of the origin of Narnia. One of the most beautiful passages in all 'The Chronicles of Narnia' describes Aslan the lion singing creation into being. Different sounds and notes result in the appearance of every feature of the world: stars, land, plants, animals, etc. The effect on those around who love Aslan is almost unbearable wonder and delight. I wonder if the psalmist experienced something similar of God as she poured out thanksgiving following all her difficulties.

What does it mean for the Lord to be your song?

LAKSHMI JEFFREYS

Love of God's law

Give me understanding, that I may keep your law and observe it with my whole heart. Lead me in the path of your commandments, for I delight in it. Turn my heart to your decrees, and not to selfish gain. Turn my eyes from looking at vanities. (NRSV)

Many years ago I helped to lead a church youth group. We used to meet on Sunday evenings for 'teaching' sessions and on Friday evenings for social activities. (After we caught a mackerel when sea fishing, I discovered a recipe for mackerel with gooseberry sauce – happy days!) The overall leader considered it important to learn Bible verses by heart, and we devised games to help do so. After all, what we focus on and remember determines our actions.

Not only is Psalm 119 the longest in the book of Psalms, but it is also written as an acrostic: each Hebrew consonant covers eight verses and, if you read Hebrew, is like a code. Reading through the verses slowly gives me a picture of someone simply sitting with God, listening to God's voice, enjoying composing and engaging with what she hears and writes. She realises she is not yet fully formed but is learning and growing; this causes her to rejoice, repent and then praise God.

The psalm is a meditation on 'God's word'; but that phrase does not simply mean the Bible. Instead, the psalmist considers God's law as interpreted and experienced. True wisdom is recognising God's voice among the many, and shaping life and worship accordingly. We worship God, not the Bible. For Christians, Jesus is the Word made flesh. Jesus knew the scriptures (the law of Moses and the prophets) and constantly used them to worship God and teach his followers, as can we.

Learning Bible verses by heart with the youth group was important. Living fully in Christ, whether fishing for mackerel, going out to work or doing a weekly shop, is what ultimately matters. Full lives are informed by the Bible, are infused by the Holy Spirit and enable us to flourish in Jesus' name.

Loving God, teach me to use the Bible to know and worship you, to grow in wisdom and to live life in all its fullness.

LAKSHMI JEFFREYS

A time to pause

I lift up my eyes to the hills – from where will my help come? My help comes from the Lord, who made heaven and earth. He will not let your foot be moved; he who keeps you will not slumber. (NRSV)

Often used in weddings and funerals because it speaks of 'my help', yet with a corporate element too, originally today's psalm was sung by pilgrims on the way to the temple in Jerusalem. I envisage one of them catching sight of the temple and, as they do so, becoming overwhelmed by a sense of God's care and protection. The terrain is dangerous, but they are seeking to worship. The Lord will defend them from external threats and will keep their soul from evil.

Psalm 121 is a favourite of mine for the evening: the day has not ended and there might be work, meetings or social activities to come, yet there is a desire to pause and reflect on experiences of God so far during the day.

It is different for women who work shifts. A friend of mine is a nurse, and I am conscious of the changing window of time when I can contact her, regardless of whether she is working during the day or at night. (Coming from a family of doctors, I am well aware of the need to let tired people sleep!) Having initially entitled this reflection 'an evening prayer', I realised the times people pause are often determined by their circumstances. But it is becoming increasingly clear to me that it is essential for everyone to have opportunities to pause and reflect, if only for a minute or two.

When walking the dog before our evening meal, I often have a moment when I am not playing with her (or trying to stop her from eating something she shouldn't). For that instant I enjoy looking around me and reflecting on how Jesus has been with me so far. Mothers with toddlers might find similar space in the bathroom!

Do you know the location of, and how to use, your personal pause button?
LAKSHMI JEFFREYS

Look back to look forward

May those who sow in tears reap with shouts of joy. Those who go out weeping, bearing the seed for sowing, shall come home with shouts of joy, carrying their sheaves. (NRSV)

Have you ever had 'one of those' weeks/months/years? You might remember 2016, when it seemed that every day someone of national or international significance died. As I write this, my family is gradually emerging from several months involving different losses – death, divorce, change, illness, etc. Certain days I managed well; other occasions I did not.

Some people seem to be defined by tragedy – someone or something they love has gone, whether through death, divorce, war or other disaster – and every aspect of life is seen through that lens of personal bereavement.

On the other hand, I think about Alice who, while caring for one elderly parent and mourning the death of another, was diagnosed with a life-threatening condition. Her husband worked away from home for weeks at a time, and the children were at critical stages of their education. Yet if you met Alice, she would always have time for you and, unless you knew her extremely well, you would have no idea of the personal burdens she carried. What was her secret?

I wonder if our psalm today offers a clue. The writer and her community have known what it feels like when the Lord brings hope out of despair. In their current suffering, they look back in thankfulness so that they can look forward with hope, knowing that God is with them regardless of their circumstances.

Thankfulness is the antidote to bitterness. It takes enormous courage not to fall into despair when life continues to be tough on all sides. One coping mechanism I have is every night to write down at least five things for which I thank God. Not only does that day come into perspective, but as I look back at where Jesus has been, I also have more faith for the future.

Someone said, 'Suffering makes you either bitter or better.' How can you give yourself the choice?

LAKSHMI JEFFREYS

Returning

From the depths of my despair I call to you, Lord. Hear my cry, O Lord; listen to my call for help! If you kept a record of our sins, who could escape being condemned? But you forgive us, so that we should stand in awe of you. (GNT)

Like many people, I can be hard on myself. Sometimes I have messed up and need forgiveness; on other occasions I wonder if I wallow rather too much in how dreadful I am. A friend with whom I pray regularly holds out her hand and says, 'Lakshmi, give me the stick.' She wants me to stop beating myself up in how I talk about what I have done; instead, I can be honest about what needs to change and ask the Lord to help me.

Repentance from sin is simply turning back to God after recognising that I have put myself first. Perhaps it is no coincidence that the central letter in sin is 'I'. While I speak about how awful I have been, I remain at the centre. When I look to Jesus and remember all he has done to bring me back to full relationship with God, other people, creation and myself, my own words, thoughts and actions come into perspective. God is always more ready to forgive than we are to turn back. That is both wonderful and humbling.

Today's psalm has an image of the soldiers on duty at night urging on the arrival of daybreak. The release from being on guard, the opportunity to relax, someone else to be in charge – all of these come to mind as the psalmist likens sentries to God's people awaiting forgiveness and restoration.

It is possible that this psalm, too, was sung as pilgrims approached the temple in Jerusalem. There is something so helpful about recognising who God is when we are worshipping with other people. While personal faith and confession are vital, we should not underestimate the power of being put right with our sisters and brothers in Christ as we repent alongside one another.

Forgive us our sins as we forgive those who sin against us.

LAKSHMI JEFFREYS

Let go and let God

Lord, I have given up my pride and turned away from my arrogance. I am not concerned with great matters or with subjects too difficult for me. Instead, I am content and at peace. As a child lies quietly in its mother's arms, so my heart is quiet within me. (GNT)

What is the opposite of worry? I put this question into a computer search engine and the first answer that came was 'mindfulness'. This has been a buzzword for a few years, and in lots of ways it makes sense. Someone who is mindful can focus on what they are doing, where they are, as they are. On the other hand, the worried individual is so concerned about something or someone else that they are unaware of what or who is around them.

One of my greatest joys in life is cuddling babies. Growing up, it seemed that our house was full of infants, since many of my parents' peers were grandparents when I was at school. From the age of about ten I discovered ways to rock babies to sleep. There was little more satisfying than a beautiful, squirming, squeaking bundle of humanity giving up the fight to stay awake and gently dropping off.

As a result I have no problem visualising the baby in our psalm, content in its mother's arms, having had all its needs met. So many women I know long for such peace, but are weighed down with concerns about family, finances, loneliness, looks, the state of the world and myriad other issues. Our worries are significant, but our minds do not need to be overwhelmed. Instead, we can learn to trust God for our needs, allowing ourselves to be held at peace in God's love.

Corrie ten Boom survived life in a concentration camp and became an internationally renowned Christian leader. She discovered that 'worry does not empty tomorrow of its sorrow, it empties today of its strength'. Her response was in a book entitled: *Don't Wrestle, Just Nestle*.

Jesus told his disciples not to worry about food or clothes, the staples of life: God would provide if they looked for the kingdom, where God is in charge.

LAKSHMI JEFFREYS

Prayer of realisation

Where could I go to escape from you? Where could I get away from your presence? If I went up to heaven, you would be there; if I lay down in the world of the dead, you would be there. (GNT)

'I prayed, but it didn't work.' People cry out to God, at times in hope and on other occasions in despair, but it seems what they want does not come about. Perhaps the problem is not the prayers themselves. Sometimes the person praying has lost sight of, or maybe has yet to encounter, the God to whom the prayers are addressed. God can become for some a parental figure, who tells them what to do yet does not fulfil their needs. And there are other people, aware of God's power, who cannot believe this God is interested in someone's daily existence. In each case, prayer can feel like putting a request in a slot machine which does not deliver.

Assuming David wrote this psalm, here was a man well acquainted with the God he addressed in prayer. Yet even David is overwhelmed by God's intimate knowledge: the God who has on countless occasions rescued his people from their enemies; the God whose name is so special it cannot be spoken; this God knows every action, thought, hope and word of David – or of you or me.

My relationship with my mother was complex. Neither of us was able effectively to express love for the other. Several years ago on a training course I attended, the leader read aloud Psalm 139 slowly; she invited us to close our eyes and allow God to speak to us. As I listened, the Lord reminded me of how he formed me; I began to imagine my mother's excitement and anxiety in pregnancy and childbirth with no close family in the country and in the days when fathers were not present at the birth. Subsequent conversation with my mother about this was beautiful and healing. I discovered answers to my deepest unarticulated prayers.

The God who created the universe speaks to you and to me in intimacy and love.

LAKSHMI JEFFREYS

Trust and power

**Don't put your trust in human leaders; no human being can save you.
When they die, they return to the dust; on that day all their plans come
to an end. (GNT)**

When my niece graduated from the University of London, two famous people received honorary degrees. The first delivered such an eloquent acceptance speech that the individual who followed could not compete. Instead, acknowledging the wisdom of what everyone had just heard, he exhorted the gathered graduates: 'The world is currently being run by cartoon characters. Please do better.'

There is constant discussion about the inability to trust politicians and leaders in almost any sphere of life. Those in authority say so much and deliver so little. Contrast this with the psalmist's experience of the God he praises. Reflecting on God's creation of the world, the psalmist concludes by listing God's protection, healing and practical care for individuals and communities.

Perhaps the difference between the way God exercises power and authority and what we see in people is *intention*: God desires the world and all creation to flourish. Jesus came to bring life in all its fullness. The fruit and gifts of the Holy Spirit bring healing and restoration of relationship within and between all created beings. While the best human leaders want other people to live well, it is impossible to expunge all self-interest or self-protection. Even within our family, I confess that decisions I make do not always have others' best interests at heart.

Sometimes trust requires understanding and experience. My son had an accident, badly bruising his foot. The nurse was outstanding but then told us we needed 'rice'. Questions filled my mind: should I cook it or pour grains on his foot? And why? She saw my confusion and explained the acronym: Rest, Ice, Compression, Elevation. Ah, understood! Now I trusted her advice.

---

*Loving God, teach us to remember your deeds, to trust your words and to
walk with Jesus in the power of the Holy Spirit.*

LAKSHMI JEFFREYS

Cosmic intimacy

He heals the broken-hearted, and binds up their wounds. He determines the number of the stars; he gives to all of them their names. (NRSV)

The Bible is the story of God restoring all of creation, including humanity. Today's psalm remembers how God returned the chosen people to their land after exile. More importantly, the psalmist reminds us of the character and nature of our God whom we know through Jesus. Think about it for a moment: Jesus was present at the start of everything, when the world began. The cosmic creator, the one who laughed, cried, taught and loved those among whom he lived to the point of death; the God who knit you together in your mother's womb and painted the sky; the God who has loved you through whatever you have experienced in the past and will remain with you whatever happens in the future; the architect of the world was the baby in the crib, born in obscurity. Centuries before Jesus was born, the psalmist and God's people knew God's love and God's special care for the poor and vulnerable.

This care is not simply for God's people: Christians are called to love the lost, the lonely, the last and the least, whoever they may be. It is relatively easy to buy an extra tin of beans to give to a food bank; it is harder to spend time with someone sleeping on the streets, to learn their name and treat them with the respect that God shows us. A friend was in town with her ten-year-old daughter when a man, sitting on the pavement, asked for money. They offered a drink instead and he opted for hot chocolate. My friend was about to choose the cheapest option when her daughter said, 'You would buy me a luxury version with cream and marshmallows. Shouldn't we do the same for him?'

How do you view God's creation, including other people?

As we listen to God, we might discover that we are the answer to our own prayers. When asked why God didn't stop war, evil, famine and homelessness, the wise minister answered, 'God did something: he created you and me.'

LAKSHMI JEFFREYS

Praise God!

Praise him with trumpet sound; praise him with lute and harp! Praise him with tambourine and dance; praise him with strings and pipe! Praise him with clanging cymbals; praise him with loud clashing cymbals! Let everything that breathes praise the Lord! (NRSV)

How appropriate that our last psalm encourages everything that has breath to praise the Lord. But what happens when we don't feel like giving God praise?

The week before I left home and work to train for ministry, a drunken man tried to break down the door of my flat at two o'clock in the morning. It later transpired he was so intoxicated that he had the wrong place, but at the time I was terrified. This was the final episode after a summer of horrible incidents. I was fed up with God for making life so difficult. In a toddler-like state, I told the Lord I would turn up at compulsory worship and lectures and undertake all the tasks I had to, but I was not going to communicate with him other than formally.

The result of hearing the Bible read every day and joining in with corporate praise and worship was that (to my annoyance!) I learned huge portions of scripture and discovered more about Jesus than I might otherwise have done. By December, I could no longer keep up the nonsense. With tears and stomping around, I poured out my feelings of anger and sadness, while recognising that the Holy Spirit had been working in, around and through me at every stage. The discipline of praise which I had endured for weeks suddenly became mine to enjoy in a new way.

The day after tomorrow will be the anniversary of my mother's death; I have a complicated funeral to conduct and an essential meeting to attend. My feelings are all over the place; reciting Psalm 150 restores perspective. I invite you, regardless of your circumstances, to declare this psalm aloud, where possible with other believers, and hear God's word to you.

'It is our duty and our joy at all times and in all places to give you thanks and praise, holy Father, heavenly king, almighty and eternal God' (Church of England Holy Communion service).

LAKSHMI JEFFREYS

Love, light and truth:
1, 2 & 3 John

Christine Platt writes:

Love, light and truth are the key themes of John's three letters. How much our world needs all of these right now to counteract the onslaught of hate, darkness and lies. Last year in New Zealand, we endured a horrific terrorist attack motivated by irrational hatred and bigotry. In the midst of the ghastliness, there was a tremendous outpouring of love and compassion towards the victims and their families. That reminds me of the beginning of the gospel of John, 'The light shines in the darkness, and the darkness can never extinguish it' (1:5, NLT). At times the contrast between love and hate, light and darkness, truth and lies is stark. That attack was one of those times – but the light still pierced the gloom.

John wrote these letters during the latter part of his life, possibly around AD85. The culture was different to ours, the causes of unhappiness and distress were different, but the answer is the same. We need more of God's love, light and truth in our world today. The wonderfully reassuring news is that God, as our amazingly generous Father, will supply all the compassion, insight and wisdom that we need to live as his people in this broken world.

I love that we have these letters written by John, who was not only an eyewitness of Jesus' life but also one of his best friends. He writes with genuine knowledge and understanding, so we can rely on his account of what it means to know the man Christ Jesus, Son of God. Think back to what you remember about John from the gospel accounts. He was a young fisherman called by Jesus at the beginning of his ministry. He spent three years listening to, learning from and loving Jesus. He was present at Jesus' transfiguration and at the cross. Jesus entrusted his mother into John's care. He was called 'the disciple Jesus loved' (John 13:23). After his apprenticeship he served God with wholehearted devotion for the rest of his days.

So we have the privilege of learning from a knowledgeable, authoritative, personal friend of Jesus as we seek to navigate our way through life in this 21st century. Although written 2,000 years ago, the life lessons he shares are timeless and relevant to today. So, let's go!

Who is this man?

From the very first day, we were there, taking it all in – we heard it with our own ears, saw it with our own eyes, verified it with our own hands… The infinite Life of God himself took shape before us. (MSG)

I'm currently reading a fascinating book by John Ortberg entitled *Who Is This Man? The unpredictable impact of the inescapable Jesus* (Zondervan, 2012). The author traces the influence of Jesus on human history in the last 2,000 years. Whatever you thought you knew, there is much, much more!

John, our elderly apostle friend and companion in these notes, gives his take on who this man is: 'the infinite Life of God himself took shape before us' (v. 2). What we think about Jesus colours everything – our approach to daily life, to relationships, to death and to eternity. There are some who would reduce him to a prophet or a wise teacher, both of which are true, but he is so much more.

Jesus himself questioned his disciples on what they understood about his identity. Peter hit the jackpot. He declared that Jesus was not John the Baptist reborn, or Jeremiah or another of the prophets, but he was 'the Christ, the Messiah, the Son of the living God' (Matthew 16:16). For a Jewish person who had grown up believing that God was unapproachable and that only the high priest could enter the holy of holies to draw near to God once a year, this must have blown Peter's mind. The idea that God would come to earth in human form and mix with ordinary people was utterly contrary to any other god and anything he had previously thought. It bears testimony to the suppleness of Peter's mind that he could put aside his presuppositions and be willing to think the unthinkable.

We can all fall into the trap of trying to reduce Jesus to limits we feel comfortable with. Whatever we think, he is much bigger, wiser, more compassionate, more outrageous and more kingly than anything we can conceive.

Lord, open my eyes, my heart and my mind to more of your wonderfulness. Help me to pray bigger prayers and to act with audacious faith in an inexhaustible Saviour.

CHRISTINE PLATT

Entering God's presence

**If anyone does sin, we have an advocate who pleads our case…
Jesus… He himself is the sacrifice that atones for our sins – and not
only our sins but the sins of all the world. (NLT)**

I've recently been reading Leviticus. There is chapter after chapter about
various offerings to bring to God – burnt, grain, fellowship, sin and guilt –
most of which required an animal or a bird, without defect, to be burned
on an altar. You get the impression that there was always some sacrifice
or other going on. The pervading smell of blood and roasting meat would
have hung in the air, giving the people the constant reminder that they
could not blithely enter God's presence. There was an elaborate procedure
to perform before they could even hope to be accepted.

This image of slaughter, blood and burning gives us a deeper glimpse
of what Easter is all about. I know how bad I feel when I realise I've committed a sin – when I've lied, been unkind or not forgiven someone. When
I think of Jesus, who'd never known what it is to feel guilt or shame, taking my sin and all the billions of sins of all the people who've every lived
and inviting all that muck on to his pure soul, it's unimaginably ghastly.
And yet, it's incredibly beautiful as well, that he would do that out of love,
though the cost to him was unfathomable.

The atonement, that Jesus paid the price for our sin, is a mystery that
we won't plumb the depths of until we meet him face-to-face. But it is a
magnificent truth and not one to be taken lightly. It is not a case of 'God
will forgive me, it's his job' (Heinrich Heine). It is that God will forgive me
because he is merciful; Jesus is my advocate who pleads my case before
the Father, and he has taken my sin upon himself.

---

*Use the hymn 'Rock of Ages' as a prayer of thankfulness that Jesus has
opened up the way into God's presence: 'Nothing in my hand I bring, simply
to thy cross I cling' (Augustus M. Toplady, 1740–78).*

CHRISTINE PLATT

Say no to cravings

Do not love this world… For the world offers only a craving for physical pleasure, a craving for everything we see, and pride in our achievements and possessions. These are not from the Father. (NLT)

John affirms all his readers, from the newest believer to veterans in the faith. He assures them that he is confident they are saved and are growing to know God. However, as a wise pastor, he knows temptation is ever near. Satan won't bother with lukewarm believers but will make every effort to trip up those who are actively pursuing God. Our enemy uses the world's ways to do his evil work.

Many things around us are exceedingly appealing. Advertisers spend billions to tempt us to buy, buy, buy. I've just been researching something online, and the number of ads that leapt up at me is nauseating. It's tempting to think I need or even deserve a tropical holiday right now, and that life will not be complete without it.

Craving physical pleasure leads to some harsh, dark places – infidelity, eating disorders, addictions, overwhelming debt. I'm sure we've all experienced how temptation starts small but grows exponentially once we give it house room.

What gives me hope is following Jesus' example when Satan tempted him: 'No! The Scriptures say…' (Matthew 4:4–11). I aim to keep some verses in mind to help combat the thoughts that Satan throws my way, such as: God will provide all I need (Philippians 4:19) or, this craving is not too strong, God will help me overcome it (1 Corinthians 10:13).

Taking some physical action also helps. 2 Timothy 2:22 says: 'Run from anything that stimulates youthful lusts' (or older-age lusts!) Let's tone up our self-discipline muscles. Use the off button on the TV or computer when you need to. Walk past the ice-cream or chocolate counter. Resist laziness. Prioritise the really important things – time with God, family and helping others come to faith in Jesus.

What temptations is Satan using right now to hinder your spiritual progress? Find some relevant verses, write them up somewhere and decide how you and God together will combat this attack.

CHRISTINE PLATT

Deception and lies

I am writing to you not because you don't know the truth but because you know the difference between truth and lies. And who is a liar? Anyone who says that Jesus is not the Christ. (NLT)

As mentioned, one of the key themes of John's letters is *truth*. The church in John's time was being influenced by false teachers. A major falsehood they promoted was that Jesus was not God. The divinity of Jesus is the foundation of our faith. Without that solid base, we are lost. Only a perfect, holy sacrifice was eligible to pay for our sins. Without Jesus, forgiveness is an impossible dream. John goes as far as to call these false teachers antichrists, even though outwardly they may have appeared to be knowledgeable and helpful people.

Prophecy warns us about the Antichrist (capital 'A') who is coming (v. 18). However, before him other antichrists will come, and are already here, who aim to deceive God's people and lead them astray. John reassures us that we know the difference between truth and lies because we have received the Holy Spirit, also called the Spirit of truth (John 16:13), who teaches us everything we need to know.

False teaching is initially presented in a subtle way, just a slight adjustment to the truth. Remember Eve in the garden – 'Did God really say...?' (Genesis 3:1). But it is powerful. I've seen mature, committed Christians get sucked in and disappear into the bog of deception. It's tragic to witness how that affects not only themselves but also their families and friends. None of us is immune. So how can we protect ourselves?

John stresses the need to 'remain in fellowship with Christ' (v. 28). To help us in this, we need to remain in fellowship with other believers whom we trust and also do our homework, like the Bereans who 'searched the Scriptures day after day to see if Paul and Silas were teaching the truth' (Acts 17:11).

Praise Jesus that he is the one and only Son of God and he is fully God and fully human. This is a key verse to learn: 'So the Word became human and made his home among us' (John 1:14).

CHRISTINE PLATT

Light a candle

You know that Jesus came to take away our sins, and there is no sin in him… The Son of God came to destroy the works of the devil. (NLT)

The Swiss theologian Karl Barth (1886–1968) said: 'Take your Bible and take your newspaper and read both. But interpret newspapers from your Bible.' Nowadays we might take in our news via radio, TV or our phones. Whichever way we absorb it, if we don't interpret it through the Bible, we are likely to become deeply depressed and cynical.

This statement – Jesus came to destroy the works of the devil – is an antidote to all the horrific news we hear.

There is so much that is sad and ghastly, but glorious events are also happening. Just imagine for a few moments if Jesus hadn't come to destroy the devil's work. Don't dwell on it; you'll feel like giving up! But if there was no goodness in the world pushing back the tide of evil, if Jesus hadn't inspired humanity to follow his teaching and example, who would be pioneering in caring for the vulnerable – the sick, orphans, refugees? What would be the place of women, and especially girl babies? The list goes on. We know there remains much to do. Satan still wields his horrific influence, but his filthy hands are tied and his power is limited.

It's inspiring to log on to websites like Tearfund, Mercy Ships and other charities and learn about their amazing work. They may never be featured on a daily news programme, but I'm certain they are headline news in heaven.

What about us? Jesus destroyed the work of the devil on the cross and he calls his followers to bring his light and goodness into our world – with our family, friends, workmates and neighbours and further afield. God's life is in us. Let it be shown to a world in dire need.

It is better to light a single candle than to curse the darkness. What can you do today to bring light and hope to those around you and to lift their burdens?

CHRISTINE PLATT

When is enough, enough?

Dear children, let's not merely say that we love each other; let us show the truth by our actions... Even if we feel guilty, God is greater than our feelings, and he knows everything. (NLT)

Love is an empty word unless it reveals itself by acts of care and compassion. But how much action is enough? We're surrounded by multiple needs and innumerable opportunities to care and to give. It can be overwhelming and exhausting. Compassion fatigue can weigh heavily on us, as yet another request comes for funds from a charity doing vital work among the needy and marginalised. Our hearts grieve for them. We want to help, but we can't give to every noble effort to relieve the world's pain. Even in our family and community, there is always more one could do. We've probably all seen people get burned out by giving and giving, until there is nothing left.

John gives godly advice here: 'Even if we feel guilty, God is greater than our feelings, and he knows everything' (v. 20). An oversensitive conscience can render us prone to overextending ourselves. That may be necessary in the short-term and God can strengthen and enlarge us to cope, but it's not generally a lifestyle one can maintain. God knows our hearts and whether true love for him is there, and he doesn't ask more than we can give.

I tend to feel I ought to do more, give more and pray more, and often beat myself up about my shortcomings. But God doesn't do that. He knows my heart and that I do sincerely want to love and serve him, and he also knows all about my limitations. I'm slowly learning to be content with what he enables me to do and leave the rest to his tender care. I love Jesus' affirmation of the woman who poured expensive perfume over his head: 'She has done what she could' (Mark 14:8) – and not what she couldn't. And he loved her for it.

Lord Jesus, help me to do what I can to serve you and your people with all my energy and resources this day and to be content. I leave all the unmet needs in your capable and compassionate hands.

CHRISTINE PLATT

Watch out! False teachers about!

My dear friends, don't believe everything you hear. Carefully weigh and examine what people tell you. Not everyone who talks about God comes from God. There are a lot of lying preachers loose in the world. (MSG)

Being sceptical is sadly now a vital prerequisite for survival in this world. More and more people are getting caught out by scammers. Even intelligent, reasonable adults get drawn in, convinced they will receive wealth or love, only to be disillusioned, disappointed and dispossessed. It's a tragic reality that we all need to approach life with a suspicious mindset. The only time humanity could wake up each morning and embrace a trustworthy world was in the garden of Eden. Those days are long gone. We live with the effects of the fall. Here, John warns us to also have a questioning attitude towards those who speak about God.

Even in our recent history, eloquent and persuasive leaders have exploited people's search for meaning. They twist the truth and influence their followers to such a degree as to alienate them from their families and take their money and possessions – all in the name of God.

But as believers, we do have some stupendous extra help to enable us to discern who is speaking the truth and who aims to lead us into error; we have the Spirit of God and the word of God.

Careful, regular study and meditation of God's word under the guidance of the Holy Spirit will form a protective barrier against false teaching. If you hear something that doesn't sound right, check it out with a trusted Bible teacher and make sure others are also on their guard. It's a balancing act to remain open to new understandings while at the same time being wary of false teaching. The Holy Spirit promises to guide us into all truth (John 16:13).

Holy Spirit of God, I so need your help and guidance to think and act rightly and to know whom to trust. Help me to be receptive to your promptings.

CHRISTINE PLATT

To be loved and to love

This is the kind of love we are talking about – not that we once upon a time loved God, but that he loved us and sent his Son as a sacrifice to clear away our sins and the damage they've done to our relationship with God. (MSG)

Every week I wait with great anticipation for the next episode of 'Call the Midwife' on TV. I love it! It depicts midwifery services in a disadvantaged area of east London in the 1950s/60s. There is one common factor in nearly all the case histories. After the trauma and agony of childbirth, the baby is placed in its mother's arms. The mother's face softens from exhaustion to utter joy. Love is instantly evident for this babe who has done nothing to earn or deserve it. That love will be tested throughout childhood and teenage years, but at its beginning it gives us a glimpse of God's love for us. 'He loved us' when we had certainly done nothing to make ourselves the least bit lovable. He offered up Jesus for us, without any guarantee that we would respond positively to his love, or even say, 'Thank you.'

Being rejected is a ghastly emotion. I'm sure all of us have experienced it to some degree. God feels it deeply too. I can't imagine the hurt and anguish that God must feel when his love, which was demonstrated at such a cost, is ignored and hurled back in his face. Yet he continues to love.

John goes on to say that 'well-formed love banishes fear' (v. 18). If we accept God's love, we need have no fear of whatever happens in life or, more crucially, in death when we come face-to-face with God's holiness. His love covers us, surrounds us and protects us. The only possible response to such immense love is to love God in return and for that love to flow out to other people. 'First we were loved, now we love.'

To truly love others, we need to know more of God's love for ourselves. If you are struggling to express love, ask God to fill you again with the realisation of his immeasurable love for you.

CHRISTINE PLATT

Bring the world to its knees

Every God-begotten person conquers the world's ways. The conquering power that brings the world to its knees is our faith. The person who wins out over the world's ways is simply the one who believes Jesus is the Son of God. (MSG)

One of the first verses I learned when I came to faith in Jesus was: 'Whoever has the Son, has life; whoever rejects the Son, rejects life' (v. 12). I loved its simplicity – if you have the Son, you have life: no Son, no life. That gave me a solid foundation stone to build on. I quickly discovered that although following Jesus may be simple, it is certainly not easy. To my amazement, John states that God's commandments are not at all troublesome. I have found some of them very troublesome! What did John mean?

John asserts that if we love God and look at life from his perspective, obedience naturally follows. In contrast, if we look longingly at the world's values and practices, it becomes increasingly difficult to walk in God's ways. The key is our faith – 'the conquering power that brings the world to its knees' (v. 4). If we trust that God is good and has our best at heart, we will follow him anywhere, as many faithful believers have done.

The world doesn't understand Christian belief in Jesus, especially if it means embracing suffering or even martyrdom. It doesn't comprehend why believers put self aside and serve the world's poor at heavy personal cost. It doesn't grasp why Christians forgo luxuries in order to support missionaries in far-flung places they will never visit. And why would you spend precious time reading the Bible and praying? The Christian life is countercultural. What makes us different is our faith that Jesus, Son of God, came to earth to rescue us because he loves us so much. Faith in our all-powerful, all-loving Jesus is the force that makes the world sit up and take notice.

Start each day by remembering and reaffirming just how much Jesus loves you, and use that conviction as a stepping stone for your choices throughout the day.

CHRISTINE PLATT

Big bold prayers

We are confident that he hears us whenever we ask for anything that pleases him. And since we know he hears us when we make our requests, we also know that he will give us what we ask for. (NLT)

God appeared to Solomon in a dream and gave him carte blanche to ask for whatever he wanted. 'What do you want?' he said. 'Ask, and I will give it to you!' (1 Kings 3:5). To his credit Solomon humbly asked for wisdom to govern the people of Israel. He was already king, but knew he could not do the job alone. Solomon's request pleased God and extraordinary wisdom was given.

John encourages us to pray for what will please God. Making us rich and famous and having stress-free lives would not be top of God's agenda for many of us. But praying for friends and family to come to Christ for salvation is a dead cert to please him. He also cares deeply about people who suffer deprivation in any way – those who are hungry, unjustly treated or homeless.

I'm aiming to develop the habit of remembering before God those who lack sufficient food. When I thank God for my meals, I ask his help for families whose cupboards are bare. I may not see the results of my prayers, but I can be certain that he hears and answers. He may also prompt me to be part of the solution by supporting my local food bank and other nutrition efforts.

This is a lavish invitation from our all-powerful, all-loving and generous God. I sometimes ask myself whether my prayers are big enough for such a God or whether I am limiting him to small projects. He says: 'I am the Lord, the God of all the peoples of the world. Is anything too hard for me?' (Jeremiah 32:27).

The Swiss theologian Karl Barth (1886–1968) said, 'To clasp the hands in prayer is the beginning of an uprising against the disorder of the world.' Let's do it!

What do you want from God today? Make your prayer big, bold and pleasing to him. Confidently expect God to answer in his time and in his way.

CHRISTINE PLATT

Spread the joy

My dear congregation, I, your pastor, love you in very truth… I can't tell you how happy I am to learn that many members of your congregation are diligent in living out the Truth, exactly as commanded by the Father. (MSG)

It sounds like John was having a ball in his job as a pastor. His life was filled with God's grace, mercy and peace, and the church was thriving. Sadly this is not always the case. Recent research among American pastors indicated that 40% of them report a serious conflict with a parishioner at least once a month, and 91% have had some form of burnout in ministry because of overwork and stress. This is an indictment on God's people.

Hebrews 13:17 says: 'Be responsive to your pastoral leaders. Listen to their counsel… Contribute to the joy of their leadership, not its drudgery. Why would you want to make things harder for them?'

We know that none of us is perfect – and that includes our pastors. As a younger Christian, I was shocked and disappointed to discover that one of my spiritual leaders had feet of clay. Later, I realised I'd put him on a pedestal where he had no right to be and certainly didn't want to be. I had expected my leader to shine in every area and virtually walk on water. The writer to the Hebrews puts the emphasis on us to contribute to the joy of their leadership and not make life difficult.

How can you contribute to your pastor's joy? John's delight came from seeing his congregation live out the truth and love one another. How is your life before God? Are you living out the truth or are there areas you'd rather people, especially your pastor, didn't know about? Are there people you struggle to love? Repent, and ask God to cleanse every part of your life and fill you with his love for people.

Make a promise to pray regularly for your spiritual leaders, that they would know God's grace, mercy and peace, and also have joy in their service for God. Why not send a note of appreciation to them?

CHRISTINE PLATT

Forewarned is forearmed

Many deceivers have gone out into the world. They deny that Jesus Christ came in a real body. Such a person is a deceiver and an antichrist. Watch out that you do not lose what we have worked so hard to achieve. (NLT)

The recent road death statistics in New Zealand are appalling. Some drivers and passengers have not grasped the message of wearing seat belts. How often do people need to be warned of catastrophic consequences? And how often do I need to be reminded to obey warnings that are given, like 'Slow down, sharp bend ahead'! Humanity is slow to learn. We tend to think we are bulletproof. We glibly assume it won't happen to us. One thing is certain – followers of Christ are targets for deceivers and we need to take heed.

As a wise pastor, John returns to this theme of warning against false teachers. One prominent lie at that time was that Christ came into the man Jesus at his baptism and left him before he was crucified – thus denying that Jesus was fully God and fully man.

John was an attentive shepherd to his flock, acutely aware of the dangers surrounding them and deeply concerned that they would not be ignorant of Satan's schemes to deceive and undermine (2 Corinthians 2:11). John realised that one warning was insufficient. He was passionately determined that they remain focused on the truth and not be sidetracked by deceivers. 'Be diligent so that you receive your full reward' (v. 8). It's not clear what reward a life of faithful service and devotion will bring, but God is the giver of rewards and that makes them worth attaining. I yearn to hear God say, 'Well done, Christine!' (Luke 19:17).

The sad fact is that there are many deceivers around us. Have you recognised them? Some may be well-intentioned, but nonetheless misguided. They try to recruit others to follow their teaching. We need to recognise the danger and be on our guard. Those younger in the faith are particularly vulnerable.

Do you have any pastoral responsibility for younger believers? Are you covering them with protective prayer and warning them against negative influences?

CHRISTINE PLATT

Companions in spreading the truth

They set out under the banner of the Name, and get no help from un-believers. So they deserve any support we can give them. In providing meals and a bed, we become their companions in spreading the Truth. (MSG)

For over 15 years, I had the privilege of being supported financially to serve God in Africa and the UK. I had a real sense of my donors being companions with me in spreading the truth. Without their help, I couldn't have done it.

John's friend, Gaius, was a generous host to travelling missionaries. I wonder if he was a bit envious of his guests. Sometimes missionaries receive extra honour and those who stay at home feel a bit inferior. This is another lie of the enemy. We are all companions together in spreading the truth, whatever our role.

Comparing ourselves with others is very human, but ridiculous. The apostle Paul was exceedingly frustrated when believers started taking sides between Apollos and him. He states: 'We each carried out our servant assignment... What makes [our servant jobs] worth doing is the God we are serving' (1 Corinthians 3:5–9). No contribution carries more prestige than another.

Those whom God calls to leave paid work need our support. I remain so grateful for supporters who enabled me to stay in Africa and also for those who provided bed and board with open arms when I was on home leave.

My church in New Zealand has an extensive outreach among youth in the community, some of whom are completely messed up. I feel totally at a loss as to how to connect with them, but our church youth workers do a magnificent job in assisting these young ones to turn their lives around. Even though this ministry is beyond my personal capacity, through prayer and financial support I'm a companion in spreading the truth among these desperately needy individuals and having a part in changing their lives. What a joy and privilege!

Loving Father, please help me to carry out my servant assignment from you with wholehearted enthusiasm. Thank you that I can be a companion in spreading the truth both at home and to the uttermost parts of your world.

CHRISTINE PLATT

Choose your epitaph

Diotrephes, who loves to be the leader, refuses to have anything to do with us… Everyone speaks highly of Demetrius, as does the truth itself. (NLT)

In his concluding words John contrasts two men – Diotrephes and Demetrius. Diotrephes sounds like a bit of a megalomaniac. He loved to be up front, the centre of attention and in charge. He refused to listen to John, even though John was the beloved disciple of Jesus himself. He denied hospitality to travelling teachers. Even worse, he wielded a malign influence on others in the church who wanted to assist the travellers and prevented them from doing so.

Diotrephes had obviously never taken Jesus' words and example seriously: 'Whoever wants to be a leader among you must be your servant, and whoever wants to be first among you must become your slave. For even the Son of Man came not to be served but to serve others' (Matthew 20:26–28). Diotrephes' idea of leadership was to assume he knew best and to boss people around.

Demetrius, on the other hand, sounds like a really good guy. He was held in high esteem by everyone, including John, who trusted him to set a good example to the believers despite the difficulty of coping with a conceited and unteachable colleague.

These few words are all we know about each of these men. It would be good to think that eventually Diotrephes recognised Demetrius' godly example and changed his ways. However, as far as we know, these phrases are their epitaphs. It seems they both served with energy and enthusiasm, but only one led a praiseworthy life.

I attended a friend's funeral this week. There was no fanfare about Geoff. He just walked with God and prayed for people. As his family talked about him, he was revealed as a man of faith, a caring husband, a devoted dad and a fun granddad. That's an epitaph worth having.

How would you like to be remembered by your peers? Think about Jesus washing his disciples' feet (John 13:1–17). Ask God to prompt you to serve others as Jesus did, with energy and humility.

CHRISTINE PLATT

Independence and dependence in God's kingdom

Michele Morrison writes:

The honeysuckle transplanted years ago coils along the dry-stone dyke, then crawls across the open ground and finally creeps up the robust trunk of a cherry tree. Fully supported, there it creates beautiful, fragrant blooms.

God wants to fully support us, so that we are free to blossom with beauty and fragrance.

In the western world, independence is a virtue to which many of us aspire. Dependence is considered humiliating, immature and irresponsible. In the context of our culture, then, how can we respond with grace and trust to God's invitation to depend on him, not as a last resort but as a first response – not just in the tough times but in our daily walk?

God, in his love for us, counsels us to depend on him in everything. Independence is intertwined with dependence: we are invited into a loving relationship with God, and, ideally, we will be so in love with him that we will make spontaneous choices which reflect his will and his character.

In John 8:31–47, Jesus declares that if the Son (Jesus himself) sets a person free, she will indeed be free. Conversely, if we are not aligned with Jesus, then we are slaves to sin. We are deceived when we declare our independence, unaware of the power the world exerts on our thinking, attitudes and actions. Any independence we claim is a mirage.

Dependence on God is the only real independence, yet I find it is a daily struggle to rely on God rather than trusting in my own detailed plans.

Jesus invites us to be yoked to him, presenting a picture of cooperation rather than dependence. In the yoking, we begin to walk at his pace, in an 'unforced rhythm of grace' (Matthew 11:29, MSG).

The war of independence was declared when Eve first picked the apple. In our pride, we are all prone to falling in on the rebels' side, which leads to disaster. Over the next fortnight, we'll be considering the relationship between independence and dependence. I hope that by the end, we conclude that, like the honeysuckle, we create our sweetest-smelling blooms when we are fully supported.

A leader who knew who to follow

Hezekiah trusted in the Lord, the God of Israel. There was no one like him among all the kings of Judah, either before him or after him. He held fast to the Lord and did not stop following him. (NIV)

How we could use a leader like Hezekiah during these uncertain times! But Hezekiah was a rare gem, unlike any leaders of Judah before or after him. He trusted. He held fast. He depended on God to save his nation.

In the opening verses of this chapter, we see that in order to serve God wholeheartedly, Hezekiah first had to dismantle existing idols on which the Israelites were depending. He was pretty comprehensive in what he abolished. 'He removed the high places, smashed the sacred stones and cut down the Asherah poles' (v. 4). Tellingly, he even broke into pieces the bronze snake God had instructed Moses to make when the Israelites were in the desert, being bitten by deadly snakes (Numbers 21:8). At the time it was made, the bronze snake served as a conduit to God's healing power, but it had become an idol and a focus of worship. Objects initially fashioned as a vehicle for connecting with God can become objects venerated as if they themselves are holy.

Last year we watched in horror as Paris' iconic cathedral, Notre Dame, was engulfed in flames. It seemed nothing could survive. The cathedral housed artworks which, perhaps, God himself once commissioned. Perhaps those precious items had become objects of worship to some. Many seem to have gone up in flames, but the next morning, astonishingly, from the depths of the destruction, a simple cross shone out. After the conflagration, the cross still stands.

Are there things in our nation's life on which we depend rather than on God? It is sobering that a touchstone with the living God can become a superstitious idol.

'Those who cling to worthless idols forfeit the grace that could be theirs' (Jonah 2:8, NIV 1984). Are you forfeiting God's grace as you cling to a worthless idol? Prayerfully consider.

MICHELE D. MORRISON

DIY weekend

All this happened because they wouldn't listen to the voice of their God and treated his covenant with careless contempt. They refused either to listen or do a word of what Moses, the servant of God, commanded. (MSG)

The fall of Samaria, seat of the king of Israel, happened because the people thought they could make their own choices. Independently minded, they ignored the Lord.

I am writing this during Easter week. I was told this morning that the secular press has nicknamed Easter weekend, 'DIY weekend'. It seems that over this weekend, most of the country heads to the home improvement stores and gets to work redecorating.

How ironic. The cross on which Jesus hung on Good Friday reveals that we cannot 'do it ourselves'. Jesus came to live and die and rise again precisely because we are unable to save ourselves from our sin; only he can. It is not DIY weekend. It is, profoundly, 'Jesus did it all' weekend.

God doesn't mind what colour you paint your walls; but he does care, passionately, about the state of your heart, and only he has the power to fix that.

How much our friends, families, communities and the nations of the world need to come into a living relationship with Jesus Christ our Saviour! He lived and died and rose again so that we can be yoked to him, so that we can cast all our care on him, so that we can utterly depend on him to guide us through the good times and the bad. We are at our best when we are clinging to him. When I am weak, he is strong (see 2 Corinthians 12:9).

DIY weekend? Only from God's perspective. When he looked at the state of us, he saw that there was only one who could truly do it for us. He had to do it himself, through his perfect, only Son: Jesus Christ.

Praise you, Jesus, that because you did it all, I can throw all my burdens on to you and have confidence that you will carry me through. I give you my anxieties now, Lord.

MICHELE D. MORRISON

Who – or what – do you trust?

So Hezekiah gave [the king of Assyria] all the silver that was found in the temple of the Lord and in the treasuries of the royal palace. (NIV)

Fourteen years after Hezekiah's demonstration of his exclusive love for God, and eight years after the fall of Israel, Judah has an enemy at the gate, attacking and capturing the fortified cities – fortified, one imagines, with walls and an armoury. Walls were not enough to keep the enemy out.

It is utterly breathtaking how completely Hezekiah has collapsed. The same Hezekiah who 'trusted in the Lord', the same unparalleled king of Judah who held fast to God, here buckles before the mighty army of Sennacherib, king of Assyria. There is no mention of his turning to the Lord now. Instead, there is a humiliating account of Hezekiah giving orders to strip the temple of all its valuables, trying to pay off this attacking force. Having once rid the kingdom of idols, Hezekiah now puts his trust in the material value of those beautiful things once dedicated to the Lord.

Despite Hezekiah's great faith in the Lord, he is persuaded by the urgent to forget the important: he doesn't go to God before responding to the enemy. He tries to save his nation in his own strength.

No amount of tribute can placate the king of Assyria, though. When he sends his supreme commander, his chief officer and his field commander to Jerusalem, they barrage Hezekiah's advisors with swaggering boasts, audaciously claiming to have come in God's name.

I find Hezekiah's failure so encouraging. I think of myself as a woman of great faith in the Lord: I can step out and speak up, lead others and even at times denounce worldly strongholds. I *can* be a woman of great faith. But sometimes when the enemy ups his game and the attack is full on, I scramble around and try to repel him in my own puny strength. Shame on me.

'Our help is in the name of the Lord, the Maker of heaven and earth' (Psalm 124:8). Lord, forgive me when I try to do it my way and don't depend on you and you alone.

MICHELE D. MORRISON

Are you tuned in to the right frequency?

'On whom are you depending, that you rebel against me?… The Lord himself told me to march against this country and destroy it.' (NIV)

That is the question, isn't it: 'On whom are you depending?' If it is on your own wisdom and perspicacity, or your bank account, or your partner… prepare to be rocked.

Hezekiah assumed he was depending on God, though there is no record that he sought God out before trying to buy Sennacherib off. In his weakened spiritual state, he might easily have been persuaded that God had deserted him. The enemy saw his weakness, and there he launched his attack. This verbal exchange is characteristic of the enemy's tactics. In the garden of Eden, he raised doubts in Eve's mind about what God really said. Here, he claims to be an agent of the God of Abraham.

It is critical that I spend time with the Lord to 'tune in' to him: to step out of the rat race, the pressure cooker, the storms of life, and to allow the Lord to recalibrate my mind, so that I recognise his voice – and also recognise the voice of the deceiver.

My family is in a time of upheaval: in my three sons' families there are three new babies and plans for relocation abroad. My daughter, speaking from personal tragic experience, is publicly campaigning for women to reject the undeserved shame of sexual assault (**#dontsilenceme**). Trying to support them all while arranging a move for my 94-year-old mother in California, I find that writing notes on independence or dependence on God is very timely. If I weren't depending totally on God now, I would be broken. But it doesn't come naturally. I am prone to listening to the voice of fear, which drives me to take charge. I have to build in times of meditative reading of the word, prayer and listening to praise music, so that I recognise God's voice and receive his peace.

Jesus said he only did what he saw his Father in heaven doing. We are to emulate Jesus, which of course we can only do through the Holy Spirit in us. It's challenging but possible, in his strength.

MICHELE D. MORRISON

Who do you go to for help?

Hezekiah prayed to the Lord… 'Now, Lord our God, deliver us from his hand, so that all kingdoms on earth may know that you alone, Lord, are God'… 'This is what the Lord, the God of Israel says: I have heard your prayer.' (NIV)

Having tried to buy off the enemy with the most valuable treasure he had – all the gems and gold dedicated to the Lord in his temple – Hezekiah's blood must have run cold to hear the taunts and claims of Sennacherib's men. The penny would have dropped if he'd had any left; still, he realises he can't do this on his own. Pride takes a knock and humility finally kicks in. He sends his cry for help to God's right-hand man on earth, Isaiah. 'Do not be afraid,' God says to Hezekiah through the prophet. Do not be afraid.

Once more Sennacherib demands capitulation, and this time Hezekiah falls on his knees before the Lord. Now at last he asks God for deliverance. Something has happened in Hezekiah. His understanding of the power and might and goodness of God has been refreshed, and he wants God to defeat this proud enemy, not for the sake of Hezekiah and his people, but for God's own sake – for the sake of his name, so that the whole world will recognise just who the Lord is.

We hear a lot about self-image. If a parent or influential person has undermined our self-worth, we can feel that we are never good enough in any challenge that comes our way. On the other hand, if we have inflated our self-image because we have been put on a pedestal for something (maybe excelling in sport, music, writing or looks), we may believe we are good enough to meet every challenge that comes our way.

We need a healthy self-image, one that recognises that only God is able to defeat our enemies. To him be the glory. Jesus promised to be with us always. Practising his presence raises our awareness of this truth.

Do you wait for a desperate situation, where your inabilities are glaringly obvious, before you go to the Lord? He beckons you. He is always waiting to shoulder your burdens with you – and share your joys.

MICHELE D. MORRISON

God says to tell you...

Then Isaiah son of Amoz sent a message to Hezekiah: 'This is what the Lord, the God of Israel, says: I have heard your prayer.' (NIV)

What an encouraging message from God. 'I have heard your prayer.' There is a sense of movement in that phrase: it's not in God's nature to hear and not to act, though it may not be in the way we hope.

God still uses prophets to communicate to us. Although all prophetic words need to be weighed up prayerfully against the revelation of scripture, I believe God uses prophecy to knit his church together into the cohesive organism he created us to be. This requires a willingness to humble ourselves and surrender to God, trusting him to speak to us and through us.

My Bible study group once challenged each other to actively seek words of prophetic encouragement for one another through the next week. As women engaged God in an intimate (and, for many, very new) way, expectantly awaiting a good word to pass on to another member of the group, they were encouraged as they recognised God's voice, and the recipients were encouraged to receive a word of love spoken over them.

Hezekiah, having initially failed to go to God, finally humbles himself and approaches the prophet Isaiah (19:2), and then falls on his face before the Lord. As he concludes his prayer, another word comes from God through Isaiah. 'I have heard your prayer.'

God always hears our prayers. That is his promise. And he acts – not always as immediately as he does in this story ('That night the angel of the Lord went out…'), but he does act. There is such beauty in a church which seeks to be surrendered to God's sovereignty and is open to his choices in the way he communicates. This is not without risk, but as we recognise our interdependence in our walks with God, Jesus is glorified in his church.

O Lord God, I surrender to you this day. I confess that I cannot live the life you call me to without you in the centre. Help me, Lord.

MICHELE D. MORRISON

War of independence?

Pray also for me, that whenever I speak, words may be given me so that I will fearlessly make known the mystery of the gospel, for which I am an ambassador in chains. (NIV)

Dependence and independence do not preclude one other. In the divine order of things, there is a synergy, almost an intimate exchange as dependence enables independence, which becomes a glorious celebration of the union between Christ and humanity. When we look at the life of Paul, we see a man exercising his free will – choosing to speak out for Christ even in dangerous situations – while depending on God's Holy Spirit and the prayers of the church. Paul is willing to open his mouth for Jesus, prayerfully trusting that the words he speaks come from God himself and are words of life. He has distilled the meaning of his life into one pure purpose: to serve God through word and deed, and he recognises that his own human frailty means he has to depend on God in order to do this. Weakness is a blessing, because in our weakness, God is strong.

Paul enlists the church to pray that the words he speaks are enlightening, godly words. This beautiful picture of interdependence reveals that as we network with the Spirit-filled church in our service to God, we are knit together into a beautiful organism, the bride of Christ.

As we soak in God's presence through worship and the word, we are changed. Dependence on God is a profound, powerful gift, which he uses to transform our hearts, minds and spirits to conform not to the world's values, but to Christ's.

Now more than ever, as politics grows extreme and divisive, and as the environment is under threat, we need to depend on God to guide us so we can lead the world back to him – not by might nor power but by his Spirit.

Do you ask for prayer support when you are in stormy waters or challenging times? If not, why not? If so, do you trust God to support you, so you move forwards with confidence?

MICHELE D. MORRISON

Share with Jesus

'Come to me, all you who are weary and burdened, and I will give you rest. Take my yoke upon you and learn from me, for I am gentle and humble in heart, and you will find rest for your souls.' (NIV)

Never was a proverb truer than the old idiom, 'A worry shared is a worry halved.' We resist being told what to do, yet we seek out solace and others' opinions when we are burdened with an issue or a difficult situation. If you choose your confidante carefully, it can be helpful to approach someone else for advice; but in my experience, others' opinions sometimes unsettle me more. It's only by responding to the invitation of Jesus, coming to him, that I feel the burden lifting. As I leave it in the hands of the one who knows everything, I can depend on him to guide me right.

I was raised to be independent; I taught that to my children. But did I learn – and did I teach – the wisdom of being dependent on God? Sadly, only perhaps as a second thought.

At a women's breakfast recently, the speaker encouraged her listeners to seek stillness with God in the midst of the chaotic busyness of life. Heads nodded in agreement as she described some of the stresses and strains of modern life. Many live with debilitating anxiety and struggle to find relief.

There were stresses in Jesus' day, too. His invitation cuts through the generations, and his words ring true today as then. I, like you, am burdened. I am weary. Having looked online to no avail, searching for people who might take my mother's household goods and furniture which would not fit in her new home, I prayed for help. Miraculously, I went to sleep, and the next day, my cousin emailed with a solution. Jesus is happy to be yoked with me as we walk my mother home. Praise him!

Depending on God is infinitely better than battling on alone.

Lord, sharing a yoke with you reminds me that you, too, have a furrow to plough. Sharing your yoke reveals your light in me, as others wonder how I can keep going with good grace. Be glorified.

MICHELE D. MORRISON

You can count on me!

'I'm leaving you well and whole. That's my parting gift to you. Peace. I don't leave you the way you're used to being left – feeling abandoned, bereft. So don't be upset. Don't be distraught.' (MSG)

Peace is more than an absence of conflict. Peace is a pervasive atmosphere within which one feels safe. Jesus' peace may not lift us out of challenging situations, but it enables us to walk through them without fear.

From where does fear emanate? Since God declares 366 times in the Bible, 'Do not be afraid', it's clear that he is not the source of fear. Fear sidles in when faith wavers, and faith wavers when we take our focus off God and become mesmerised by a situation. Instead of practising the presence of God, we are all too quick to practise the details of a problem, rehearsing possible scenarios in our minds and devising ways to arrive at a solution.

It feels irresponsible to relinquish control to God. We have a sense that as responsible adults we ought to shoulder our burdens and pull our weight. But as we read yesterday, Jesus invites us to share our burdens with him, to be harnessed with him. What happens when we make a determined decision to yield control to God? Opportunities open up for us to see him in action, miracles in the making.

As I shared yesterday, different aspects of my mother's pending move have given me concern. When I've brought them to the Lord, I've watched him provide solutions. When I awake in the night anxious, I try to focus on God. Last night he enabled me to get back to sleep twice as I relinquished my urge to strategise and gave control to God. 'On my bed I remember you; I think of you through the watches of the night' (Psalm 63:6, NIV). Far better to focus on him than on the problem.

Lord, transform my mind. May I develop a healthy dependence on you, receiving your peace and recovering the joy and fullness of life you promise us.

MICHELE D. MORRISON

I can do it

'My Father, if it is not possible for this cup to be taken away unless I drink it, may your will be done.' (NIV)

My parents said that as a child I would often shake off offers of help with the declaration that I could do it by myself. One of my grandsons, Gregor, at age two, fiercely grabbed his spoon at mealtime and said, 'I do it.' There is nothing wrong with a healthy self-confidence when it comes to mastering some of the skills required in life. The beauty of life lived in the Spirit is intertwining our own abilities and gifts with the will of God.

We see this rich beauty revealed in Jesus' life. As the gospel accounts show, Jesus chooses to return to Jerusalem, fully aware that the knives are out for him there. Jesus does not return to Jerusalem in ignorance of what awaits him, yet in his interaction with his Father in the garden of Gethsemane, he still begs that this cup of horror be taken from him. This is a beautiful, poignant picture of independence intertwined with dependence. Jesus' says these loving words of surrender to the Father he trusts implicitly: 'Your will be done.'

Did you notice that the first time Jesus petitions his Father, he asks, 'if it is possible' (v. 39), and the second time, resigned, he says, 'if it is not possible' (v. 42)? Nowhere do we see more clearly the meshing of Jesus' human with his divine nature. It seems impossible that any of us mere humans could follow Jesus along this road to martyrdom, and yet history sparkles with examples of those precious disciples whose unshakeable allegiance to God led to the sword or the stake.

Persecution of Christians is vicious and fierce in our day. Many of our brothers and sisters sublimate their safety to the call of God on their lives. Pray for them now.

MICHELE D. MORRISON

Problems are opportunities

Therefore you do not lack any spiritual gift as you eagerly wait for our Lord Jesus Christ to be revealed. He will also keep you firm to the end, so that you will be blameless on the day of our Lord Jesus Christ. (NIV)

As you wait, he will keep…

As I make arrangements to relocate my mother, I am acutely aware that I am not up to the task. But God is, and he is faithful. This morning I sobbed out to him a problem for which I could see no resolution. This afternoon, a friend of my mother's offered the solution, even though I'd not approached her with the problem! The Lord Jesus Christ is revealed, and to him be all the praise, honour and glory.

I am living out the reality of being independent – investigating removal firms, arranging changes of address, figuring out where to dispose of extra furniture and which lifelong treasures to keep – while knowing that I can only do this as I depend on Christ. I especially rely on him to help my mother to be agreeable, flexible, willing to adjust to a new place full of strangers, at a time when her memory is increasingly compromised. As we wait for Jesus, he will keep us both strong to the end.

I am balancing this transatlantic move with helping my children with new babies, especially my eldest son and daughter-in-law, who live over an hour away and have a two-year-old boy and twin babies.

My unchurched neighbour Mary, with whom I walk regularly, comments that she's never known anyone with so many pressures to balance at once. My prayer is that as she watches me, Jesus Christ is revealed.

Isn't it astonishing that Paul can write with such assurance that we lack no spiritual gifts? That is not because he thinks we are amazing; it's because he knows God is amazing and he is faithful to his promises.

Lord, you allow situations in our lives which challenge and even frighten us, but as we step forward, leaning into you, you are revealed. Our problems are opportunities to see you work.

MICHELE D. MORRISON

Teamwork

When you're joined with me and I with you, the relation intimate and organic, the harvest is sure to be abundant. Separated, you can't produce a thing. (MSG)

Why do we have such a hard time accepting this beautiful picture of peaceful harmony in Christ producing a wonderful crop? Most of us can slip into Martha-mode, overwhelmed by busyness as we respond to needs all round us. We know that faith has an outcome of good works, and, perversely, that can propel us into making a to-do list of good works without nurturing that godly relationship from which the to-do list should spring. We can be suspicious of anyone having control of us: we have coined the phrase 'control freak', and we resist anyone having such power over us. Perhaps we imagine God as a control freak. Nothing could be further from the truth, for God has designed us to partner with him in stewarding his beautiful creation.

In our demanding 21st-century world, technology vibrates or buzzes or dings, calling us to check our emails, our WhatsApp, our Facebook. I have to be very deliberate in setting aside time to draw away with God. Jesus walked on the hills, sometimes all night. I am blessed to have a 'prayer window' which looks out on a pastoral landscape. The constantly changing Scottish sky adds interest, and when I step into that alcove, I sense God's presence, and my desire is to join with Jesus intimately. It is when I am pressured, as I am now, that I most crave the peace of Jesus, and as I abide in him, I receive his peace. I emerge refreshed. My eyes are open to see him act.

Jesus invites us to make our homes in him 'just as I do in you' – astonishingly interdependent. Jesus lives in me by the power of his Holy Spirit. Do we give thanks wholeheartedly, daily, for the amazing gift of God?

O Lord God, I give you thanks and praise that your love is unconditional, that you are faithful, that your generosity knows no bounds and that your mercy saves me. Thank you.

MICHELE D. MORRISON

Humpty Dumpty

Put your hope in the Lord. Travel steadily along his path. (NLT)

My two-year-old grandson Callan was playing with his toys. I could hear his voice, soft and sweet, singing, 'Humpty Dumpty sat on a wall. Humpty Dumpty had a great fall. All the king's horses and all the king's men couldn't put Humpty together again.'

Humpty Dumpty was broken beyond repair. When I look at the trashing of our beautiful world; when I see the devastation in Syria; when I listen to the heated wrangling in Parliament; when I hear of another mass shooting in America; when I see marriages coming unstuck and children growing up with no anchor – I can sink into the despair of this nursery rhyme. Nothing can put it all back together again.

But we have a God whose grace and mercy never fail. This is his world; we are his people – all of us. People never dreamed the almighty God would give his Son to live and die among us so that we might be 'put back together again'. But that's exactly what he did. He put us together so that we can partner with him in bringing light into the darkness.

People today, lost, alone and hopeless, need to hear the good news that there is one who can put it all back together again. He is the same one who raised Jesus from the dead (Acts 2), and as Peter said, 'We are all witnesses of this.' When I was at my lowest ebb, 40 years ago, Jesus came into my life and I was born again. He put me back together again.

Put your hope in the Lord. Travel steadily along his path, dependent on the Lord, but independently choosing to travel along his path. As we trust in him, we discover that he gives us the desires of our hearts.

Father God, you are faithful. Your promises are true. This is your world; we are your people. Perhaps we have never needed you as much as we do right now. Come, Lord Jesus.

MICHELE D. MORRISON

The buddy system

Let us run with endurance the race God has set before us. We do this by keeping our eyes on Jesus, the champion who initiates and perfects our faith. (NLT)

We run the race laid out for us by focusing on Jesus. It's easy to get side-tracked and charge off in the wrong direction, full of enthusiasm and our own good ideas. I've done that many times, only to face-plant into a mud puddle. It's good to remind ourselves that Jesus himself said he only did what he saw his Father in heaven doing. His human eyes no doubt saw lots of things he could do, but he resisted the temptation to serve his Father in his own human wisdom and instead relied on the wisdom from above.

How do we do this, day after day, for a lifetime? How do we endure? By leaning into God. When the road becomes a precipitous, steep track, then more than ever we need to lean into God and not depend on our own understanding of the situation. When I grow weary, worn down by the relentless demands and challenges, I lean in, and as the 'Footprints' poem affirms, at those times Jesus carries me. He once whispered into my heart, 'In every teardrop there is a rainbow.' I remember that and look for the rainbows.

I am amazed to watch visually impaired athletes competing in the Para-lympics. Racing blindly, fully committed, round a track or skiing down a snowy slope, they are tethered to a sighted athlete who can match their prowess and keep them on course. It's called the buddy system.

In this world, we are all visually impaired. We cannot see what is really going on, but Jesus can. By linking up with Jesus, our forever buddy, we can run with commitment and endurance the race God has set before us. Better together.

Father God, you never call us to do things without fully equipping us. In everything you enable and equip. I thank you for your precious Holy Spirit, living in me.

MICHELE D. MORRISON

Jeremiah

Lyndall Bywater writes…

Welcome to the book of Jeremiah. If I tell you that one of this prophet's favourite phrases was 'sword, famine and pestilence', you'll get the gist of what we're in for over the next two weeks!

Jeremiah prophesied for the last 40 years before Judah was conquered by Babylon and the vast majority of its people were taken into exile. Though there were some peaceful, prosperous times, he spent most of those 40 years having to take his people to task for their unrighteous, ungodly behaviour – everyone from kings and priests to the men and women in the street. Despite the seriousness of the hour and the message, there is real, solid hope at the heart of Jeremiah's prophecies, so I promise it won't all be gloom and doom.

The contents of the book of Jeremiah were written over the course of several decades, and they're put together in no particular order, so we will be jumping around a bit. I've also included a few suggestions of passages to read from Lamentations, because that set of lament poems is also likely to be Jeremiah's work. Much of the language, in both Jeremiah and Lamentations, is highly poetic, and I personally found it helpful to read the passages in more modern translations, to give me a fresh perspective. You may find that helpful too.

So why would we want to spend two weeks with a man who, while having sparkling moments of hopefulness, had an awful lot of negative things to pass on to a nation who lived thousands of miles and thousands of years away from where we are today? Very simply because Jeremiah is about being honest, facing hard realities, speaking uncomfortable truths, confronting injustices and helping people to find hope. We may not be in imminent danger of occupation by a foreign power, but we certainly have our fair share of painful realities to face up to, both social and political, and a whole host of injustices which may go unchecked unless we, the church, have the courage to speak out against them. And, of course, our world needs to hear the message of hope just as much as it did in Jeremiah's day.

These passages may not be easy reads, but my prayer is that time spent with Jeremiah will help you to discover the unique message which God has given you to share with his world.

Made for your purpose

'Today I have made you a fortified city, an iron pillar and a bronze wall to stand against the whole land – against the kings of Judah, its officials, its priests and the people of the land.' (NIV)

A dear friend once built me a cabinet. I was off to university and he knew I would need to store lots of tapes, CDs and videos, so he designed me a bespoke portable set of shelves which would fit each of them perfectly. In this era of digital downloads, it's now sadly redundant, but I still keep it because I am ever in awe at the meticulous way he designed it and the love with which he made it.

Jeremiah was called to be a prophet. It wasn't a pretty calling. There was no golden handshake and no enticing pension offer. God was honest about the fact that it would be a hard job. He'd need to speak truth to people who didn't want to hear it and there would be tough times ahead. Admittedly, God did promise his own presence, but it probably didn't feel like much of a consolation to Jeremiah after all that talk of uprooting and tearing down.

But Jeremiah wasn't just called to be a prophet; he was *made* to be a prophet. Despite appearances to the contrary, God wasn't sending a frail, stammering, ill-equipped young lad; he was sending a young lad who he had already made into 'a fortified city, an iron pillar and a bronze wall', a perfect fit for the task.

If you find it daunting to think about what God is calling you into, try thinking instead about what he's making you into. What qualities is he growing in you? What strengths is he building? What gifts is he giving you? What do you find easier than you used to?

Whoever you are, however inadequate you feel, God has been shaping you since before you were born, and he's making you into the person you need to be to answer his call.

Take time today to ask God what he's making you into. The answer may come as words, as a picture or as a scripture that pops into your mind, or it may come through something someone else says to you.

LYNDALL BYWATER

Summing up Jeremiah

'If a prophet has a dream, he should tell others of that dream. But the one who has My word should speak it with *unshakable* faith. For what is straw *worth*, when compared to grain? Does not My word *burn* like fire? Does it not shatter rock like a *strong* hammer?' (VOICE)

At time of writing, Steve Bray from Port Talbot in Wales has been protesting outside Parliament for over three years. Dressed in his distinctive blue-and-yellow outfits, he can regularly be seen and heard in the background of media reports as he makes his one-man stand of defiance. Whatever you think of his politics, one thing is certain: Steve knows what his message is, and he's sticking to it!

God was making Jeremiah into a tenacious man who would stick to his message, and this chapter is one of the most succinct summaries of that message. It has three main strands, and each one corresponds directly to one of the phrases God used in chapter 1 to describe what he was making Jeremiah into (1:18).

First, God was making him a 'fortified city'. A fortified city is a safe place in a world of danger; it represents refuge and salvation to those who have lost hope. Although a lot of the book is rather gloomy, Jeremiah did bring some glorious messages of comfort, promises that God would again bring his people to a safe and hope-filled place (vv. 5–8). Second, God was making him an 'iron pillar'. Iron pillars are solid, uncompromising things, and Jeremiah needed to deliver uncomfortable truths to people who didn't want to hear them (vv. 16–20). Third, God was making him a 'bronze wall'. Bronze signifies judgement, and Jeremiah was certainly a champion of justice, calling out unrighteousness and exploitation wherever he found it, especially in those who held positions of leadership and trust (vv. 9–15).

We'll examine each of these three strands in more detail in the coming days, but today let's see the bigger picture. Since time immemorial, God's people have been called to speak out that threefold message of truth, justice and hope.

We're all called to share the message of the gospel, but we all have a message of our own… a particular God-truth which we carry deep within us and which we long for others to know. What's your message?

LYNDALL BYWATER

Saying it like it is

Then the officials said to the king, 'This man should be put to death. He is discouraging the soldiers who are left in this city, as well as all the people, by the things he is saying to them. This man is not seeking the good of these people but their ruin.' (NIV)

> Public sentiment is everything. With public sentiment nothing can fail; without it nothing can succeed. He who moulds public sentiment goes deeper than he who enacts statutes or decisions possible or impossible to execute.
> Abraham Lincoln

It was true in Lincoln's time, it's true in our time, and it was certainly true in Jeremiah's time: if you can control the public mood, then you have a lot of power. Jeremiah 38 refers to a time when the kingdom of Judah was in a lot of trouble. Powerful enemies were circling and defeat looked inevitable, but the prophets – the influencers of the day – were telling a different story: if everyone just held their nerve, it would all be fine and God would come through for them. Perhaps they were simply trying to keep morale high; perhaps they were looking to eleventh-hour rescues of the past to reassure themselves. Whatever their motive, Jeremiah had been sent to tell them they were wrong. There he was, the solid, unbending iron pillar, resisting every temptation to say the easy, popular thing, and it nearly got him killed.

What makes this situation different to all the other impending disasters which God turned around at the last minute? It comes down to honesty. Take King Hezekiah, for instance. He had faced certain defeat at the hands of the Assyrians just a few decades earlier, and that story had ended very differently indeed. Hezekiah was a humble man, and the rescue came only after he had poured out his heart to God in honest prayer (see 2 Kings 19:14–19). When leaders refuse to tell the truth, disaster follows. When leaders choose to be honest about things – honest with God, with themselves and with their people – then miraculous rescue is possible.

Lord, we pray for our political leaders. Give them courage to be honest about the challenges we face, give them humility to tell the truth, even when it's uncomfortable to hear, and turn their hearts to prayer.

LYNDALL BYWATER

An underwear moment

How can I understand your plight, dear Jerusalem? What can I say to give you comfort, dear Zion? Who can put you together again? This bust-up is past understanding. (MSG)

In Ken Loach's film *I, Daniel Blake*, Daniel suddenly finds himself unable to work due to ill health. To apply for benefits he has to fill in an online form, even though he's never used a computer before in his life. I claim benefits myself, so I'm familiar with the complexities, but it was agony to watch his bewilderment and desperation as he struggled with the unfamiliar technology, knowing it was the only way to get the money he needed. It broke my heart to realise in a new, deeper way that so many are struggling like that in real life.

God was making Jeremiah into a pillar of iron, a man with a hard message of truth to bring, but his inner strength didn't come from his own opinions. His inner iron was forged by deep grief at what he saw.

Films weren't available then, but God had other ways to awaken Jeremiah to the truth of things. Jeremiah 13 is a story about underwear (sometimes translated 'linen shorts', 'linen belt' or 'loincloth'), but it was also a moment when Jeremiah came face-to-face with painful reality. As he held his rotten garment, I imagine his shock at seeing what it had become, and his even greater shock as he realised what God was saying about the mess his people were in. God was calling him to rebuke them, but only after he had first felt the pain of their plight deep in his heart.

Our world needs to hear the truth of the mess it's in, but it needs that truth to be spoken by people who have had the courage to face the reality of that mess and to grieve over it. Only truth spoken out of deep compassion will ever have the power to change things.

Have you ever had an 'underwear moment' like Jeremiah – a moment when a truth has come home to you so powerfully that it's broken your heart? How has that moment changed the way you live and how you treat others?

LYNDALL BYWATER

Welcoming the tears

I wish my head were like a spring of water and my eyes like a fountain of tears! Then I could cry day and night for my people who have been killed. (NCV)

I was in the middle of a speech, and, if I may say so, it was rather a good speech. It was nothing formal, just a bit of a rant to my friends on a topic I feel passionately about, but I was flying, right up to the moment when my throat closed up, my eyes began leaking and I started to cry. So embarrassing… so frustrating… and yet so much more common as I get older.

When we think of Jeremiah being made into an iron pillar, it gives the impression of someone cold and hard-hearted; someone who has long-since suppressed all their emotions for fear of being seen as weak; someone so focused on their task that nothing can move them anymore. You only have to get a few chapters into his book to realise that's not the kind of iron God was forging in Jeremiah. This prophet was anything but hard-hearted. He had some hard truths to expose, but his messages weren't delivered with cold detachment; they were full to bursting with strong emotions. And this was a man who cried often. If you like, Jeremiah was an iron pillar with a built-in fountain.

God is making you into something – maybe not an iron pillar, but something equally unique and beautiful – and the more you become what he's making you, the more passionate you get about the things that matter to you. If you were thinking age and maturity might help you pack away those awkward emotions, the ones that take your breath away when you're trying to be measured and coherent, then I'm afraid you might be disappointed. Emotions are an intrinsic part of being human. They are God's gift to us and he loves them, so don't be afraid to let them come.

Creator God, as I become more and more the person you're making me to be, help me to embrace my emotions, not fearing them or suppressing them, but making space for them in my life and letting others see them.

LYNDALL BYWATER

The whole truth

'For I know the plans I have for you,' declares the Lord, 'plans to prosper you and not to harm you, plans to give you hope and a future.' (NIV)

I recently saw the musical *Hadestown* on Broadway. It was profound! If you don't know, it's a retelling of the Orpheus and Eurydice myth, and though it was written over a decade ago, its themes are scarily apt for America's current political climate. I'm pretty sure most of the relatively young audience hadn't done their Greek mythology homework, though, so had no idea what a sad ending the story has. As Orpheus failed in his quest and Eurydice fell back to the underworld, there were gasps and even sobs from the auditorium. But it was in that bleak moment that the band suddenly struck up with a song about hope in dark times, and the mood shifted in a way that was deeply spiritual.

Our world needs prophets who aren't afraid to tell the truth about how things are, but it badly needs those prophets to also sing songs of hope. Jeremiah did both. In today's passage, he was again telling his people that they needed to accept the reality that they had been invaded and defeated, and that exile in Babylon was an inevitable consequence, but he also wanted them to know that God was still with them, loving them and planning for their good. He was living proof that an iron pillar, though it may be hard and unyielding at times, is also a solid place to lean when the weight of truth becomes overwhelming.

Being prepared to speak hard truths is our responsibility as Christians, but an even more vital part of that responsibility is to speak the truth about God. He is the one who allows us to live the consequences of our harmful choices, but he is also the one who never leaves us. He is the one who leads us back home to love.

What hard truth is God asking you to face today? Is it something you need to speak out about? If so, what is the truth about God which you also need to speak out, to add hope to your song?

LYNDALL BYWATER

Power matters

'But he was just and right in all his dealings. That is why God blessed him. He gave justice and help to the poor and needy, and everything went well for him. Isn't that what it means to know me?' says the Lord. (NLT)

I get to speak in all kinds of churches, and if I ever need an illustration which I know everyone will relate to, no matter what denomination, I just mention 'the cup cupboard'. If this is a new concept to you, the cup cupboard is the sacred place in a church where a certain set of cups is kept. They're very nice cups, all of the same pattern and with matching saucers, and they're usually reserved for the sole use of the women's group. The cup cupboard generally has a key, and that key is often kept by someone formidable.

How we use power matters. Today's passage is a collection of Jeremiah's messages to various kings of Judah, men who feathered their own nests and exploited the poor, and though that kind of tyranny may seem a million miles from the cup cupboard, it's all about how we use and abuse power.

God was making Jeremiah into a bronze wall (1:18). In Hebrew tradition, bronze signifies judgement. God was asking his prophet to call out injustice and wrongdoing, and some of his harshest judgements were against those who used their power to abuse and control the powerless.

God even went so far as to make a direct link between handling power well and knowing him. If we use our power to care and to bless, then we've found the meaning of knowing him. Presumably therefore, if we let power go to our heads and we use it to control or oppress others, we can't truly know him. That's a sobering thought.

The kings Jeremiah was speaking to were afraid of invasion. Perhaps that's why they used their power so badly. Do you have a 'cup cupboard' – a situation in which fear is making you cling to power and use it to control others?

You may not have the cup cupboard key, but we all have power: the power to affect the lives of others for good or ill. Ask God to show you what power you have and how to use it well.

LYNDALL BYWATER

Judgement begins with the house of God

'Do you really think you can steal, murder, commit adultery, lie, and burn incense to Baal and all those other new gods of yours, and then come here and stand before me in my Temple and chant, 'We are safe!' – only to go right back to all those evils again?' (NLT)

Passages like these are hard to get a handle on. If you're taking time to read these daily Bible notes, you're probably someone who wants to live a good, godly life, and you're unlikely to be murdering anyone or worshipping Baal any time soon. So what can we take from this?

This passage is likely a judgement God gave Jeremiah to speak shortly after the death of King Josiah. Josiah had undertaken a huge temple clean-up, getting rid of everything that offended God and making it a place of true, honest worship. But after his death, the rot set in again very quickly. Before long, the priests were back to their old ways of mixing temple worship with all kinds of wrongdoing – and those priests were probably Jeremiah's relatives. He wasn't a religion-hating outsider; he was the son of a priest. Yet God had made him into a wall of bronze, someone with the courage to shine the light of justice into the darkest corners of sin and depravity. He must have hated seeing his family and that precious, beautiful temple being brought into disrepute, but he knew that the injustice had to be exposed so it could be stopped.

It's a sad reality that the church today is better known for its wrongdoing than its 'rightdoing'. As the light of justice is shone into dark corners of secrecy, coercion, abuse and even brutality, scarcely a week goes by without the media finding another story of how powerful people in the church have betrayed its most vulnerable members. Maybe we'll never need to speak out like Jeremiah did, but we do need to persevere in prayer, asking the Holy Spirit to reveal hidden wrongdoing and to help us build a fairer, kinder, safer, more just church.

Holy Spirit, we pray for your church. Search us and know our hearts; test us and examine our thoughts. Point out anything in us that offends you, and lead us along the path of everlasting life (based on Psalm 139:23–24).

LYNDALL BYWATER

It's always personal

'But I, God, search the heart and examine the mind. I get to the heart of the human. I get to the root of things. I treat them as they really are, not as they pretend to be.' (MSG)

Have you ever been falsely accused? Perhaps it happened because someone misunderstood something you did or said and ended up jumping to a conclusion about you that was just plain wrong. It's moments like that when you wish you could show your accuser the inside of your heart, so they'd know what your motives and attitudes really were.

Jeremiah was one of the first ever to talk to God's people about having a personal relationship with him. It's hard to believe that, given how much there is in the rest of the Old Testament about many of our faith heroes relating to God in such a personal way, but most of those stories were only written down at least a century after Jeremiah. Jeremiah's writings are some of the earliest in the Bible, and what he had to say about the heart – that personal relationship with God – was new and radical at the time. Until then, people had tended to think that God looked on them as a community rather than as individuals. Perhaps that's why some of the leaders thought they could get away with so much unrighteousness, because God wasn't really looking that closely.

The bad news for them was that God was indeed looking that closely. And he is still looking that closely today. If that worries you, be encouraged: your inner life may not always be as spotless as you'd like it to be, but when you're planted by the river of God's grace, trusting in the forgiveness he offers you in Jesus, your heart is constantly being washed clean. And the even better news is that, when you feel misunderstood, you can take comfort from the truth that there is one who sees your heart and who knows it completely.

Is there someone you're annoyed with? Have you perhaps misunderstood something they've said or done? Ask God to talk to you about the good things he sees in their heart. That often makes it easier to forgive and move on.

LYNDALL BYWATER

Non-negotiables

'The command that Jonadab the son of Rechab gave to his sons, to drink no wine, has been kept, and they drink none to this day, for they have obeyed their father's command. I have spoken to you persistently, but you have not listened to me.' (ESV)

The Rechabites were a little nomad clan who, thanks to a pledge made by one of their ancestors, had lived for 200 years as teetotal tent-dwellers, never drinking alcohol, never growing crops and never building houses. They had come into the promised land at the same time as Israel and had remained friends ever since.

When Jeremiah invited the Rechabites to meet with him, Hebrew culture would have required him to offer them food and drink, and they would have been glad of this, since they weren't self-supporting, so they relied on the generosity of others to survive. It must have been a shock, then, when Jeremiah offered them nothing but wine. I have some sympathy for them: I've been part of the Salvation Army all my life, so I know what it's like to turn up at a party, dying of thirst, only to find there are no decent soft drink options available!

Jeremiah's lack of hospitality may seem rude, but in fact he was using the situation to hold them up as a shining example of faithful obedience. For them, drinking alcohol was a non-negotiable. God had made Jeremiah a bronze wall to call out the wrongdoing of his people, and he was grieved by the fact that, unlike the Rechabites, they didn't seem to have any non-negotiables anymore. He had no issue with alcohol, but he did have an issue with his people's refusal to listen and obey their God.

We humans tend to find non-negotiables tricky. We either become inflexible about things that don't really matter, or we fear offending people, so we shy away from having strong opinions about anything. But non-negotiables are a sign of a healthy inner life, providing we make sure we're non-negotiable on the things which matter most to God.

Is there someone you admire because of a stand they've taken? Pray for them, for strength to hold their ground. Ask God to help you reflect on your own non-negotiables. Are you holding tightly to the things he values most?

LYNDALL BYWATER

God is good

'Let the one who boasts boast about this: that they have the understanding to know me, that I am the Lord, who exercises kindness,
justice and righteousness on earth, for in these I delight,' declares the
Lord. (NIV)

> In my own life, I think I can honestly say that out of the deepest pain
> has come the strongest conviction of the presence of God and the
> love of God.
> Elisabeth Elliot, *Be Still My Soul* (Revell, 2004)

These words become all the more remarkable when you consider that they
were written by a woman who was widowed twice in her life, the first time
when her husband, Jim, was murdered by the Amazonian tribesmen they
had come to share the good news of Jesus with. Despite the pain she must
have known, Elisabeth took her little daughter back to Ecuador and lived
among that tribe for years.

Having read some of Jeremiah's writings, you could be forgiven for
thinking he must have had a gloomy existence. Being forged into iron and
bronze, having to share hard truths and confront injustices, he had much
to feel sad about, and with all the talk of punishment and destruction, he
could easily have had no other message than warnings of God's wrath. Yet
suddenly we find him reciting the goodness and kindness of God. He had
learnt what Elisabeth Elliot would later learn, that even in the depths of
despair, God's love and presence cannot be snuffed out.

God was making Jeremiah into a 'fortified city' (1:18), and a fortified
city is a safe place. In all the upheaval, God didn't want his people to have
a distorted view of himself, so Jeremiah was tasked with helping them to
know who God truly was – not a cruel, cold-hearted destroyer but a fair
and kind father who wanted his children to be fair and kind to one another.
No matter how dark the times may become, God never ceases to be good.
He never ceases to love us and show us kindness.

---

*Do you remember a dark time when you were aware of God's love and pres-
ence? Take some time to reflect on it. What did you learn about him? How did
that experience change the way you think of him now?*

LYNDALL BYWATER

God is at work

'So I went down to the potter's house, and I saw him working at the wheel. But the pot he was shaping from the clay was marred in his hands; so the potter formed it into another pot, shaping it as seemed best to him.' (NIV)

I love to sew, and I particularly enjoy making clothes for myself. As well as being a relaxing pastime, it's helping to cure me of my perfectionism. You see, I might start out aiming to make a dress, only to cut the fabric wrongly and find I suddenly don't have enough for the garment I'd planned. In the early days, I'd throw the lot away in bitter disappointment, but now I just reroute my plans and make a top with the fabric that's left.

God was making Jeremiah a fortified city, and fortified cities are very comforting places to be when everything seems to be coming down around your ears. This little story of the potter is tucked in among many a prophecy of doom, but it served to remind Jeremiah's listeners that God had not entirely given up on them; he was the potter who could make and remake and remake the work of his hands. Even after all the mistakes they'd made, if they would only return to him, he would be able to make them into something new.

Such is our desire to get things right for God that we sometimes forget his grace. We strive for perfection, then beat ourselves up for falling short, only to assume we've blown it altogether. But the master potter always has us in his hands, working around our failings and smoothing over our shortcomings, and he shapes us as seems best to him. He knows how to make us the very best we can be.

Do you ever feel like you are pottery gone wrong? Perhaps you've made a mistake, or circumstances have knocked you out of shape. Put your trust in God and stay in his hands. He will make you into something you never imagined you could be.

Do you know someone who feels like everything has gone wrong? Pray for them today, that they will know grace and hope. You could even send them a message of encouragement to reassure them that God is still at work.

LYNDALL BYWATER

God can do anything

Then the word of the Lord came to Jeremiah: 'I am the Lord, the God of all mankind. Is anything too hard for me?' (NIV)

'The Wall' is a sculpture celebrating answered prayer. It will be made of one million bricks, and each of those bricks is sponsored by someone who has a story to tell of having seen God act in response to their prayers. Building has been taking place throughout 2020. As I read the story of this unusual project, what encouraged me most was the fact that many people have bought bricks in faith – they haven't seen the answer to their prayers yet, but they believe they will, so they've bought a brick as a statement of trust in God.

Having spent years and years warning his people that they were going to be taken into captivity, it must have come as something of a surprise to Jeremiah when God told him to buy a field in his hometown. Surely, if God was to be believed, there'd be nothing left of that hometown in years to come. But Jeremiah's words weren't just the iron of reproach and the bronze of judgement, they were the rock-solid walls of a fortified city – a reminder that there would be rescue and restoration in years to come. Having prophesied disaster, he bought that field in a very public way, to reassure his people that disaster would not be the end of the story.

To pray is to push against the tide. It's important that we acknowledge the painful realities of life, but that doesn't mean we have to let those painful realities have the last word. Nothing is impossible for our God, and that means we turn to prayer, looking beyond the brokenness and asking for the restoration. Even in the midst of chaos and captivity, Jeremiah was praying for the return of God's people to their promised land – and that's what happened.

Father God, thank you that disaster is never the end of the story with you. Help me to see resurrection. Help me to pray for the things which, though they seem impossible to me, are not impossible for you.

LYNDALL BYWATER

Closer than ever

'I will put my law in their minds and write it on their hearts. I will be their God, and they will be my people. No longer will they teach their neighbour, or say to one another, "Know the Lord," because they will all know me, from the least of them to the greatest.' (NIV)

We've reached the very heart of Jeremiah's message – the pinnacle of that fortified city of hope which God had made him into – and it is one of the most breathtaking views in all of scripture. The words in the second part of today's reading are probably very familiar to you, since they even made it into the New Testament (Hebrews 8:8–11), but try to imagine how astounding they would have been to the people listening to Jeremiah. They'd never been told before that God wanted a personal relationship with each one of them. Up to that point, the relationship with God had been mediated through corporate acts of worship and priestly rituals. The idea that everyone would actually know God, from the least to the greatest, must have sounded scandalous. The priests would be out of a job, for a start!

And that truth is still utterly life-changing today. Whoever you are, whatever you've done, wherever life has taken you and wherever you find yourself today, God longs to have a personal relationship with you. He wants you to know him, not by reading books or asking Bible teachers, but by spending time with him. He wants you to know his voice, share his thoughts, soak up his love and enjoy his presence.

Do you ever spend ages trying to work out the right thing to do in a particular situation? Do you ever find yourself asking, 'What would Jesus do?' The amazing truth of Jeremiah's message is that you won't always have to wonder; you won't always have to agonise about whether you're getting things right. One day you'll know. You'll know God so well that it'll become completely natural to live life his way. That is God's promise to you and his gift to you in Jesus Christ.

Knowing God seems like a huge undertaking, but that process has already begun in you. Stop for a few moments now and think about God. What do you absolutely know about him, in the deepest part of yourself?

LYNDALL BYWATER

Women of the New Testament

Diana Archer writes:

Off the top of your head, how many New Testament women could you name without looking at your Bible?

There are so many, including the famous and not-so-famous. There are those who regularly appear in church's stained-glass windows – like Mary the mother of Jesus – and others whose names you might struggle to remember or even recognise, like Nympha. Who do you relate to? Are there any you don't? Whose stories do you know? Do you have favourites?

Depending on how well we know the New Testament, and where we are on the Christian journey, we will be able to name more or fewer women. I imagine that many of us will know about Mary and Martha, Jesus' friends in Bethany, who were the sisters of Lazarus. We may have clocked Mary Magdalene too, who was part of the crowd of disciples following Jesus. We probably have our own ideas stored of other women who feature in memorable stories – like the woman who was dragged before Jesus and a crowd of men for judgement, having been caught out in adultery.

We may have heard that the way Jesus treated women was revolutionary in his time. This is reassuring, as it looks like the men had more of the fun. It was men whom Jesus called to be his disciples, wasn't it? Those twelve names are definitely male. Against a backdrop where a significant part of our contemporary world is trying to bring equality of treatment for women with men, it is hard for some of us to get our heads round the first-century Jewish understanding of women counting for 'less' than men. Yet much of our world still has a similar view, and women are abused more than men in every way,. While we may have to learn to appreciate the particular ways that this applied in Jesus' time, the principles are comparable to today's situations.

Therefore the encounters that Jesus had with women, and the ways that women operated in the early church, are all the more precious – not just because of the larger issues of equality but also because of the everyday troubles and joys that these women faced. Just like us. We are considering women who lived two thousand years ago, but I am willing to bet that you, like me, will find that you relate to every single one.

A woman of Samaria

Jesus replied, 'If you only knew the gift God has for you and who you are speaking to, you would ask me, and I would give you living water.' (NLT)

We begin with one of the fascinating women, immortalised in the New Testament, whose story you probably recognise. It took place as Jesus' extraordinary ministry was taking off. The Pharisees, Jewish religious leaders of the day, were beginning to take umbrage, and so Jesus avoided conflict by leaving Judea and returning to Galilee.

Tired by the journey, he broke convention by asking an unknown woman at a well in Samaria for a drink – a man speaking to a woman, alone, was not done. Drawing water in the worst heat of the day indicated that her chequered past and lifestyle meant she was not welcome with the crowd at cooler times. However, this unlikely woman took Jesus on – perhaps she was used to fighting for herself – and argued back with this unusual Jewish man who had scant regard for social taboos.

Yet Jesus must have seen in her a deep longing. He plunged into a provocative discussion with her, ranging from her theological objections to Jewish worship, to the nature of spiritual water versus water from the ancient well. He threw in his God-inspired knowledge of her; and he challenged her to discover who he was. He offered a tantalising picture of never-ending water, a 'fresh, bubbling spring… giving… eternal life' (v. 14). He got under her defences, so that she ran back to the village to summon everyone, bubbling herself with the excitement. Had she met the long-awaited Messiah?

Do not imagine that your doubts, questions, theological wrestling or moral failings are too difficult for Jesus. Jesus meets us just where we are, in the daily-ness of life; he is up for every question; he understands our quest for fullness of life; and his offer of himself as living water is still the same.

Read John 7:38–39. Find out the gift God has for you.

DIANA ARCHER

Ms Canaanite

'Have mercy on me, O Lord, Son of David! For my daughter is possessed by a demon that torments her severely.' But Jesus gave her no reply, not even a word. Then his disciples urged him to send her away. 'Tell her to go away,' they said. 'She is bothering us with all her begging.' (NLT)

Talking of arguing back, check out this Canaanite woman. This is one of the slightly awkward stories in the Bible. What was Jesus thinking, not even replying? Then, when he did speak, it frankly sounded rude. Yet Ms Canaanite did not flinch. She would not be put off getting help for her daughter.

First, no matter what the commentaries say, there is no easy way to read this. Was Jesus testing her faith? Was he wanting to draw out a response that showed others how deep her belief in him actually was? She had addressed Jesus as 'Lord, Son of David', despite not being Jewish herself. Somehow, she knew that Jesus was special. She saw him.

Second, she did not care about how she looked. She was going to get Jesus' attention no matter what stood in her way. She went for it.

Third, Ms Canaanite was driven by her love for her daughter. Those of us who care for children, one way or another, know this feeling: if our children are threatened, there is nothing we will not do to protect and help them. Ms C. persisted against the discouragement of all those male disciples – who really were rather insulting and dismissive of her – and had a ready retort for Jesus' reminder that his first duty was to Israel. She believed that Jesus could help her, and a bit of verbal and theological jousting was a small price to pay.

I wish I could have seen the look on Jesus' face. The impression given by 'Dear woman', as Jesus responded to her (or 'Good answer!' in Mark 7:29), implies that he had been smiling all along. He was delighted with her faith. He pronounced her daughter well. He went to a predominantly Gentile area next, to bring the kingdom of God.

Don't be afraid to be honest with Jesus. He can take it. Just try and see him for who he is.

DIANA ARCHER

A woman determined

For she thought to herself, 'If I can just touch his robe, I will be healed'… And he said to her, 'Daughter, your faith has made you well. Go in peace. Your suffering is over.' (NLT)

This is one of my favourite stories. I love that it recognises the misery of long-term physical problems and the implications that can result. This poor woman had been in discomfort, and perhaps pain, for so long. Not only that, but she was ritually 'unclean' in the eyes of Jewish law because of the continuing blood flow: her social life and her spiritual life were curtailed, and her family life as well, for you had to be 'clean' to eat with others, to be touched and to take part in the community. And while there may have been good, hygienic reasons for that, it certainly affected her life badly in every way.

I love that she was another determined lady who focused on getting to Jesus. She did not want any drama; she just wanted a chance of being healed. She must have sneaked through the crowd, head down, knowing she was pushing the boundaries of social acceptability to get to him.

I love that she was filled with fear when Jesus insisted on finding her. Not for her the clever answers or arguing back. She wanted to slip away with her body intact at last. But Jesus had more to give: he affirmed her faith and declared her 'clean' in the sight of all. Her touching of Jesus did not make him unclean too; rather, in the topsy-turvy way of the kingdom of God, it made her clean instead.

Jesus saw it all – saw her fear, her courage, her suffering, her persistence, her hope and her despair. He met her just as she was and honoured her in front of a pushy, noisy, excited crowd. It was an exceptional act of affirmation and restoration. This is what he does. Let him do the same for you.

Dear Jesus, there are times when I feel I am struggling to get to you through all the things that would stop me. Help me to connect with you and hear your voice today.

DIANA ARCHER

A woman caught out

Then Jesus stood up again and said to the woman, 'Where are your accusers? Didn't even one of them condemn you?' 'No, Lord,' she said. And Jesus said, 'Neither do I. Go and sin no more.' (NLT)

This is one of the ultimate examples of Jesus' treating women with honour, compassion and care in the midst of a patriarchal, law-bound society.

How dreadful to be 'caught in the act'. Jewish law demanded the evidence of two witnesses, so it must have been pretty dramatic. Why didn't they drag the offending man in front of Jesus too? This, however, was not the first or last time that a woman has been condemned and used; here, the point of all this was to entrap Jesus. The accusers did not care a fig about the woman. They just wanted to ensnare Jesus – they wanted to catch *him* out.

They should have known better. Jesus was never fooled, nor outwitted. Here, he responded by taking the heat out of the situation. He bent down to write in the dust. And yes, we all wish we knew what he wrote and why. Then he neatly turned the tables again, inviting only the sinless to fulfil the law and fling the first stone.

If you have ever been 'caught in the act' in any way, or know that you were lucky not to be, then you will appreciate the remarkable balance of justice and compassion that Jesus achieved here. He and the woman were left, still surrounded by a quiet crowd, but with no accusers. He gave her life back to her, literally, including the invitation to a new start. Did she look in his eyes before she scuttled away? Did she see that Jesus was rescuing her from shame as well as death? Was this her life-defining moment? Did she even begin to follow him? I hope so. I hope that she saw in Jesus her way out from escapist behaviour and her way in – to eternal life.

Let us give up our foolishness of trying to find happiness in crazy ways. Let us take Jesus at his word and build our lives on that.

DIANA ARCHER

A woman with perfume

When a certain immoral woman from that city heard he was eating there, she brought a beautiful alabaster jar filled with expensive perfume. Then she knelt behind him at his feet, weeping. Her tears fell on his feet, and she wiped them off with her hair. Then she kept kissing his feet and putting perfume on them. (NLT)

Am I the only one who relates to this story on a visceral level? When I am filled with gratitude to God for the gifts of every day, or so glad to receive forgiveness yet again, I do wish that I could do this – to show my appreciation in physical, meaningful and honest ways. I want to wrap up a big present, or buy a beautiful bunch of flowers to give to him.

Is that a bit girly for you? What would you do? If you had been this woman, so aware of how rubbish your life had become, so upset that Simon was treating this extraordinary Jesus so carelessly, so overwhelmed by the forgiveness and love you saw in him – what would you have done? Would you have thrown convention to the winds, in like manner, and covered his feet with perfume and kisses?

This is a story of gratitude and passion, and we see Jesus' trademark response of compassion, acceptance and affirmation. In contrast, Simon was horrified. He could not believe that Jesus would allow such a woman to get near him. But Jesus elevated this woman of ill repute way above the 'respectable' Simon. He willingly accepted her extravagant gesture and her love. He encouraged her repentance and declared her forgiven, saved, at peace. Yet again, he upended the social norms for the sake of one woman who was prepared to be honest about her need.

This is who Jesus is. For the sake of the one, he will drive through niceties, expectations and taboos. For the sake of the one, he will ignore the popularity stakes and what the perfectionist law-keepers think he should do. For my sake. For your sake.

How do you best show your love to and for Jesus? How do you best receive his for you?

DIANA ARCHER

Procula

Just then, as Pilate was sitting on the judgment seat, his wife sent him this message: 'Leave that innocent man alone. I suffered through a terrible nightmare about him last night.' (NLT)

How did Matthew know about this? Did a Jesus-following servant overhear the conversation? Did the messenger tell all, and the titbit found its way back to Matthew? My favourite idea is that Pilate's wife became a believer later and told the story herself. Not a new thought, as it turns out, for it found favour with the third-century theologian Origen; indeed, the eastern and Ethiopian Orthodox Churches have canonised her – named Procula – as a saint. They further suggest that Pilate became a convert too.

Procula's dream was part of the drama of those dreadful days leading up to Jesus' unmerited crucifixion. Pilate was struggling with a city seething with unrest, Jewish subjects who were ramping up the tension, and no matter how he tried to delegate responsibility for Jesus' fate, it kept coming back to him. The news of his wife's dream would not have helped. He knew already that he was in a no-win situation.

Have you ever had a time when you can see that things are going wrong, and you try and fix it, and it still goes belly-up anyway? Procula (if that was her name) must have felt like that. She had no power to wield, but she did what she could. She tried to influence her man, but it did not work. She could see a great injustice about to take place but could not stop it. She must have been so frustrated and distressed.

And God must have seen her. Whatever that dream was about, wherever it came from, God's plans were bigger than she could possibly have dreamt – which is why I really hope that she came to understand, in the end, that he can bring the greatest hope out of the greatest disasters.

Dear Father, it is so hard to trust you when life goes badly wrong. Please help me to look up at you in those times.

DIANA ARCHER

Mary Magdalene

Thinking he was the gardener, [Mary] said, 'Sir, if you have carried him away, tell me where you have put him, and I will get him.' Jesus said to her, 'Mary.' She turned toward him and cried out in Aramaic, 'Rabboni!' (which means 'Teacher'). (NIV)

One of the arguments for the validity of the accounts of the resurrection in the gospels is the fact that they don't match very well. Luke has Mary going to the tomb with Joanna, Mary the mother of James and others; Mark includes a Salome; Matthew has 'the other Mary' too.

The point is that eyewitnesses very rarely tell exactly the same story. Those who have made up a tale together are more likely to 'get the story straight'. This is well recognised in courts of law. The point for us is that we can trust these accounts: in those chaotic, scary, unexpected days post-crucifixion, when the disciples were reeling with shock and grief, the last thing they expected was some women telling them that they had seen Jesus alive again. It is a glorious piece of history that it was to the women, or woman, that Jesus entrusted his resurrected self. These second-class citizens, whose word was not even accepted as testimony in the courts, were honoured by being the first to hear the greatest news of all time.

It is so easy to imagine oneself there – blinded by grief, shaken by the absence of the body – turning around to ask the gardener what had happened. Would I have known Jesus' voice, like Mary did? What a wonderful thing that was. The impossibly good had happened, and Jesus was back. No surprise that she flung herself at him. And what of us? Do we recognise Jesus' voice in the times of crisis? Do we turn towards him, knowing he must be there somewhere? Do we listen for him calling our names, reaching out for us? Or do we stay inside the tomb, thinking we are deserted?

Dear Jesus, please help me to know your voice so well that I can hear and recognise it no matter what is happening around me – even today. Thank you.
                                                                    DIANA ARCHER

Sapphira

About three hours later his wife [Sapphira] came in, not knowing what had happened. Peter asked her, 'Tell me, is this the price you and Ananias got for the land?' 'Yes,' she said, 'that is the price.' Peter said to her, 'How could you conspire to test the Spirit of the Lord?' (NIV)

Heard any good sermons about Sapphira lately? I thought not. We are very keen on the bit about believers looking after each other and willingly contributing to each other's welfare, but what happened to Sapphira, unsurprisingly, is not so popular.

This disturbing incident took place very early in the newly birthed church's life. Things were exciting – people were believing in Jesus, healings were commonplace, the disciples were preaching to the great and the good, angels were springing believers out of prison – and the community of Jesus-followers was growing in numbers and maturity.

Then, suddenly, we read of this very sobering moment. The story is explicit in maintaining the complicity of Sapphira in this strange, mixed-up act of half-generosity. What were she and her husband Ananias thinking? No one forced them to sell their land, as Peter pointed out. Did they just want to look good in the eyes of others? Were they trying to show off a bit, or gain some status in the fledgling community? What was the point of what they did, and why did they compound the issue by lying about it? I wonder if Peter had some suspicions already – or why else would he have questioned them so directly?

What are we to learn from the fate of poor Sapphira? Is it as simple as: don't mess with God, because he sees all? If so, most of us would have dropped dead years ago. God loved Sapphira as he loves us, but the emphasis here is on the deep disloyalty of lying to the Holy Spirit. It was not so much the money as the lying, both to their community and to God. How can God work in our lives if we are not honest with him? How can we live in the kingdom of God together if we are not honest with each other?

Dear Father, help me to trust you so deeply that I do not need to manipulate or lie to you or others, to secure my future.

DIANA ARCHER

Lydia

One of those listening was a woman from the city of Thyatira named Lydia, a dealer in purple cloth. She was a worshipper of God. The Lord opened her heart to respond to Paul's message. (NIV)

I have never noticed before that God called Paul and Silas to Macedonia through a man in a dream, and when they got there, all they found were women. Thank goodness they did not leave the riverbank and go looking for the dream-man. Lydia's immediate acceptance of the gospel and her generous offer of accommodation were a glorious heart-response to the good news that Paul and Silas shared with her and others; and the new church which began that day gathered in this – presumably – Gentile woman's house. It shows that Paul's declaration, 'There is neither Jew nor Gentile, neither slave nor free, nor is there male and female, for you are all one in Christ Jesus,' (Galatians 3:28), was lived out in his own life. What a change from the traditional Jewish understanding of needing ten men to form a new synagogue. How often do we expect God to work in one way – and he does something else?

Not only did Lydia respond herself, but her household did too. Lydia was a significant member of Philippian society, clearly a successful businesswoman, trading in the unique purple cloth that was produced only there, using the local water and probably the sea-snail shells to produce the colour. Lydia sounds like the sort of person who was everyone's friend. Within days, the number of believers rocketed. Paul and Silas did not have long to be with them, for they were beaten, imprisoned and evicted from the city for causing a riot through their ministry. But it was to Lydia's house they returned when miraculously released from prison (v. 40).

The gift of hospitality that Lydia offered was crucial to the mission in Philippi – she was Paul's 'dream woman', as it turned out.

Where can you be an answer to prayer for the mission of God?

DIANA ARCHER

Priscilla

[Apollos] began to speak boldly in the synagogue. When Priscilla and Aquila heard him, they invited him to their home and explained to him the way of God more adequately. (NIV)

Some of us go to churches where all the senior leaders are men. Others of us will be mystified by this priority, surrounded by many examples of effective senior female Christian leadership, and taking for granted that women are as suited for leadership as men.

Without delving into the convictions on both sides of this debate, it is worth noting that the honour Jesus consistently gave to women during his lifetime seems to be reflected in the way the early church grew. For example, after their initial encounter with Paul, Priscilla is always named first in every mention of this dynamic Christian couple. Despite being kicked out of Rome for being Jewish, the hospitality they gave to Paul in Corinth was critical for his ministry and developed theirs as well; and again when they all moved to Ephesus. Here they encountered the influential preacher Apollos. The story makes it quite clear that it was the two of them who set Apollos' theology straight, not just Aquila.

There was a brilliant female lecturer at theological college when my husband and I were there, who sometimes remarked upon the fact that she was trusted to teach would-be church leaders, but not to be one (at that time). Priscilla taught Apollos about what he was missing – about Christ's death and resurrection, about the indwelling Holy Spirit and about the gospel being for both Jews and Gentiles. No doubt there was many a time when she, her husband and Paul had talked theology long into the night. Paul's references to this couple show that they were dear to him; he called them both his 'fellow workers in Christ Jesus' and his gratitude to them was huge (Romans 16:3).

Hospitality, theological debate, teaching, caring, friendship that took risks to protect Paul, church hosting – Priscilla placed her gifts and strengths in the service of the early church and its mission.

What are the gifts you do or can offer for kingdom-building? If you don't know what they are, then talk to a friend and find out. Let God work through you as he did Priscilla.

DIANA ARCHER

Euodia and Syntyche

I plead with Euodia and I plead with Syntyche to be of the same mind in the Lord. Yes, and I ask you, my true companion, help these women since they have contended at my side in the cause of the gospel, along with Clement and the rest of my co-workers. (NIV)

It seems a bit sad to go down in biblical history as the women who fell out with each other, but there it is. I do hope they were reconciled, for it was clearly a situation that Paul cared about.

Conflict among church members – how tricky this is. For some reason we seem to be surprised every time, I suppose because we have caught a glimpse of the extraordinary harmony that the Spirit of God can bring; the amazing fellowship that exists only between believers that is unlike any other on the planet; and the aim we all have of living 'as one', as Jesus prayed for us (John 17). We see relationships that are true, caring and unselfish, between those Christians who know they are accepted by God, so don't have to fight for their place in the world or put others down to get it. So when conflict comes, it hits us doubly hard. 'There's no pain like church pain,' as a friend once said to me, who was in the middle of it.

We do not know what the disagreement was between Euodia and Syntyche, but it looks like it was something Paul thought could be resolved. It is not always. But Paul encouraged those around them to help. It is undeniably hard at times to get past hurt and difficulties in relationships, and we often need the perspectives and support of others to make it possible. Paul reminded the women of the bigger picture – that of a world to be won for the gospel – because he knew they cared about it. Perhaps that was what called out of him the heartfelt and enduring encouragement of verses 4–9: God cares, knows and can bring peace to us no matter what we face, beyond anything we could imagine.

On Kindle, Philippians 4:6 is the most underlined verse in the Bible: 'Do not be anxious about anything, but in every situation, by prayer and petition, with thanksgiving, present your requests to God.' How do you apply it in your life?
DIANA ARCHER

Lois and Eunice

I am reminded of your sincere faith, which first lived in your grand-mother Lois and in your mother Eunice and, I am persuaded, now lives in you also. (NIV)

If we ever needed encouragement that our faith matters to our families, here it is. No matter who we are, or what our role or place in the family, our relationship to Jesus can make all the difference.

Paul was writing to Timothy to encourage him, and perhaps give him a little prod, to stand firm in his faith. Timothy was in Ephesus, and Paul, under arrest in Rome, wanted Timothy to come to him. Paul recognised that he was nearing the end of his life, and he needed to pass the mantle on to Timothy (4:5–8). He knew that this was a challenging calling, so he reminded Timothy of his heritage and security in God, beginning with his mum and granny.

Despite the wonderful encouragement of dramatic stories of conversion from those who encounter Jesus later on in life, there is nothing to compare with the privilege of growing up in a home where he is part of the family. I had such a blessing. Jesus was just around in our house: Christian values were taken for granted, and my life and perspectives were always bigger as a result. Of course, it was not perfect, but come teenage years, I knew I had the choice to opt out if I wanted, rather than opt in. While I spent many hours researching to find out if it was all true – and wishing I could have one of those dramatic conversions – I could not deny the evidence of God's presence in our family's life.

I am so grateful for this, and now I have many conversations with contemporaries about the importance of living out our faith for our children and grandchildren to see. Like Lois and Eunice, the younger ones in our lives may need our example more than we know.

Paul encouraged Timothy to 'carefully guard the precious truth that has been entrusted to you (v. 14, NLT). How do you do that?

DIANA ARCHER

Nympha

Please give my greetings to our brothers and sisters at Laodicea, and to Nympha and the church that meets in her house. (NLT)

Here we meet another woman who hosted a church in her house. Although this is all we know about Nympha, I would very much prefer to be marked throughout the centuries as a church host, rather than a woman who fell out with another.

Perhaps Nympha led the church as well as hosting it; it is not entirely clear from the context. What is clear is that Paul sent his greetings to her specifically, and then sent his greetings to the church through her, so it is reasonable to assume that she was the key person in that particular Christian community.

In the potent mix of cultures that was the world of the Middle East in New Testament times, women were often seen as possessions, ornaments and second-class citizens. However, Paul did not treat them as such. For him, they were valued co-workers for the kingdom. Despite the ongoing debates about contentious passages in his writings (for example, headship in 1 Corinthians 11 or submission in Ephesians 5), when Paul mentions women by name, it is always with respect and usually in the list of greetings to significant people in local churches.

Without wishing to dive into issues about the relative roles of men and women that better minds than mine are still discussing, I do now realise just how many women are included in Paul's writing, and, it seems, in his heart's affections. William Booth, founder of the Salvation Army, said that 'some of my best men are women'. I wonder how many women, even in the early church, were getting on with leading, enabling, growing and spreading the kingdom, in a way that has never been fully recognised. Well done, Nympha.

Read Joel 2:28–29.

DIANA ARCHER

Junia

I commend to you our sister Phoebe, a deacon of the church in Cenchreae… Greet Priscilla and Aquila, my fellow workers in Christ Jesus… Greet Andronicus and Junia, my fellow Jews who have been in prison with me. They are outstanding among the apostles, and they were in Christ before I was. (NIV)

As we come to the end of our brief list of some of the women in the New Testament, there is no better place to come into land than Romans 16. Do take time to read the chapter. Here are people who are precious to Paul, whom he wants to honour – as should we.

Just look at all the women who featured so strongly in his Christian journey. There was Phoebe, a deacon – part of the serving leadership of the church – who looked after Paul when he needed help, and to whom he was still so grateful. Priscilla and Aquila pop up again here (Priscilla first), as he thanks them for risking their lives for him and implies that many Gentile churches owe them greatly.

There was a Mary, Tryphena and Tryphosa, Persis, Julia, Nereus' sister – and Rufus' mother, to whom Paul includes a special tender note remembering how she was a mum to him. Paul may have been the most significant theologian and church planter of the early church; but even he needed mothering at times.

Then Junia. Could it really be that Junia has been hidden from us, as a female *apostle*, because some scripture transcribers somewhere, for whatever reason, changed her name to masculine? Could this 'outstanding' woman really have been misunderstood for two millennia? Incredible. If you are feeling hard done by today, think of poor Junia.

So let us not be afraid to be who we are today, as women following in the footsteps of those in the New Testament. Let us not limit our potential, or think we are not enough. We walk on the kingdom ground that was won for us by Jesus, and the women who lived in the newness and the glory of it. Let us be worthy of their example.

Dear Father, help me to see myself as you do. Help me to embrace and enjoy being just who you have made me to be.

DIANA ARCHER

God who is ever present: 1—2 Samuel

Selina Stone writes:

The Bible is full of the incredible stories of very ordinary people who say 'yes' to God and to a life of adventure. These women and men remind us that even though we may think of ourselves as insignificant and unimportant at times, God is able to imagine much more for us than we often imagine for ourselves.

We will be delving into 1 and 2 Samuel in the next couple of weeks to explore the stories of holy prophets and uncertain kings, wise women and angry giants, civil wars and family conflicts. We will come across some of the most well-known figures in Christian tradition and some of the most famous stories – it will be quite a ride. Yet, this history begins with the prayers of a crying Hannah, a godly yet tormented woman who longs for a son. In the midst of her personal pain, she could not find God at work, but at the right moment God, who has always been present, reveals himself and answers her prayer. Samuel, Hannah's son, is not just a gift to her but to the nation too, through his ministry as a priest and a prophet during this crucial time in Israel's history.

In the next couple of weeks, we will reflect on the lives and relationships of Saul, his son Jonathan and David his friend, under the theme, 'God who is ever present'. We will trace their journeys from the moment God calls them, through the highs and the lows they experience. We will watch them as they face their personal demons and reflect on how they handle external threats. We will see them make good choices and catastrophic ones, and through it all be reminded of the God who is present with them.

These reflections are designed to remind us of how God sits with us and walks with us through all of the moments of life, whether we are faithful to him or not. My prayer is that as you enter into their stories and the reflections which accompany them, you will be able to trace the presence of God in your own life, whether you find yourself in times of insecurity or hope, isolation or friendship, fear or victory.

Hiding from the call

Saul the son of Kish was taken by lot. But when they sought him, he could not be found. So they inquired again of the Lord, 'Did the man come here?' and the Lord said, 'See, he has hidden himself among the baggage.' (NRSV)

This is an interesting start to Saul's time as king. Rather than running at the opportunity to take on this role, instead he is caught hiding among the baggage. On one hand, this may seem like a humble posture to take, but on the other hand, this could seem more like a sign of insecurity and fear.

In the run-up to this moment, there have been clear signs that God has chosen Saul for this position. He leaves his father's house in search of lost donkeys and bumps into the prophet Samuel, whom God had told in advance to host a feast and to save a plate for the unsuspecting new king arriving at that specific time and place. Samuel anoints him and God confirms it through a move of the Spirit; but then by the time he gets home, Saul hides what has happened, even from his father. When all the people gather for Samuel's announcement, it is all too much for him to handle.

It is normal to feel afraid or have insecure thoughts. As human beings, we have so many voices which impact how we see ourselves, what we do and how we live in the world. Those around us can say things which hurt our self-esteem or make us question whether we can or will accomplish what we hope for. Our own internal narrative can be the most negative, reminding us of our failings, weaknesses and limitations. But the voice of God calls us, despite this, to embrace his calling to be and do something significant in this world. Even though we might prefer to hide, God will find where we are and shout to the world, 'There she is!'

In our own lives, it can be very easy to underestimate what God may be calling us to be and do. Where in your life do you think you may be 'hiding among the baggage'?

SELINA STONE

Fear: the foundation of compromise

[Saul] waited for seven days, the time appointed by Samuel; but Samuel did not come to Gilgal, and the people began to slip away from Saul. So Saul said, 'Bring the burnt-offering here to me, and the offerings of well-being.' And he offered the burnt-offering. (NRSV)

We have already noted that fear somewhat characterises Saul's behaviour, and in today's passage we see that fear never remains a personal issue, but often leaks into affecting our actions and those around us. There were always very clear guidelines for how offerings should be presented to God in the Old Testament. Samuel and the other priests were those called by God for the ministry of managing the temple and worship. But here, Saul oversteps into this very sacred role, because 'the people began to slip away'.

It is easy to understand why Saul may have felt panicked in this moment: he is in the middle of a battle and is under pressure. The Philistines are threatening to defeat the Israelites, the army are trembling and Saul is scared they will lose. They want to be sure God will grant them victory, but Samuel, the sign of God's presence and his word, has still not returned. What results is an act of compromise, and then God's decision to reject him as king and find 'a man after his own heart'.

Self-sabotage is one of the biggest challenges we can face in life. It is so easy to allow our fears to dictate our actions and to make choices in our relationships, our careers or our lives in general which compromise the good life that God desires for us. Sometimes it seems justified – we fear being alone, not having a lot of money, not being seen as successful by others. And yet, in compromising, we risk missing out on the best life that God has in mind for us as his daughters. We can often count ourselves out when things do not go according to our timeline, and we choose to go our own way. We would do well to remember that the God we know in Christ is not one who rejects us when we fail.

Loving Father, you know us completely and understand our fears, pressures and needs. Come to us afresh and do not delay, that we may live faithfully, resist compromise and see your promises fulfilled.

SELINA STONE

The last one

Jesse made seven of his sons pass before Samuel, and Samuel said to Jesse, 'The Lord has not chosen any of these.' Samuel said to Jesse, 'Are all your sons here?' And he said, 'There remains yet the youngest, but he is keeping the sheep.' (NRSV)

It seems strange to us that Jesse, when asked to bring out his sons, would forget David and leave him in the field. In many families the youngest child can often be the favourite (this is a sore point for me, being the oldest of four!), but this is clearly not the case in this family. Even after going through each of the sons and discovering that God has not called any of them, David is only remembered because Samuel asks if there are any more. Can you imagine the disbelief and surprise everyone in the room would have felt as one by one the Lord says, 'It is not this one'?

This is a wonderful and comforting story for those of us who have ever felt like the last one to be thought of, called or remembered. At different times in life, we can feel like we are out there in the fields, in those undesirable places, working hard and never being noticed. It can seem that everyone else is the likely candidate and that others are always the ones who are recognised and suggested for moves forward in life. However, in this passage, we find a God who does not choose the ones who everyone else considers to be the obvious choice. He looks past the tall, handsome brothers with the strong arms and the good shoulders, and he picks little 'ruddy' David who is probably filthy and messy and the smallest of them all. Samuel makes them all wait until David gets back from the field, and then he anoints him and gives him a seat of honour.

Whether we are the ones who get to choose others, or we are hoping to be chosen, let us hold this in our hearts today – that our God is the one who looks for the last one.

SELINA STONE

Practice makes perfect

David said, 'The Lord, who saved me from the paw of the lion and from the paw of the bear, will save me from the hand of this Philistine.' So Saul said to David, 'Go, and may the Lord be with you!' (NRSV)

David has clearly been having quite a rough time out there in the wilderness looking after sheep. Aside from battling with the elements, he has had to defend himself and the sheep under his care from lions and bears – oh my! He recognises that it is God who has helped him to survive those battles, and he sees Goliath as nothing more than another similar challenge.

It would have been perfectly acceptable for David to have been afraid – he could have considered his lack of military experience, his youth and height in comparison to the age and height of his adversary, or even the fact that it was not really his job to fight when Israel already had its armies and warriors. Yet David models a kind of childlike faith in God; he draws a very simple line from his experience of God's protection in his life so far and the current situation where he will definitely need God to be his defence. David has practised his trust in God: he has seen his faithfulness and is emboldened to take on this challenge, which even those who are twice his size are afraid of.

Trusting in God is essential to the life of faith, and can also feel like the most unreasonable thing to do. God can be unpredictable; sometimes he does not do what we ask or show up in the way that we hope. David shows us here that, rather than only being absorbed in the challenge in front of us, we have to take time to look back to find the evidence of God's faithfulness and love. Things may look pretty bad at the moment, but God has moved and acted in your life before.

Looking back over your life, note those defining moments when you saw God act in your life and in the lives of those around you. Practise remembering and giving thanks, even as you pray regarding your present challenges.

SELINA STONE

Plots and politics

Now Saul planned to make David fall by the hand of the Philistines... When Saul realised that the Lord was with David, and that Saul's daughter Michal loved him, Saul was still more afraid of David. So Saul was David's enemy from that time forward. (NRSV)

It becomes clearer as we go through 1 Samuel how the initial fear and insecurity that Saul demonstrates have catastrophic consequences for his personal relationships, as well as his leadership as king of Israel. As David's success increases under the blessing of God (which Saul is aware he no longer has), Saul's jealous anger increases to the point that he begins to plot ways to kill him. He fears David even more, knowing that both his daughter and his son love David, who is also protected by God himself.

There is something very sad about the degeneration of the relationship between David and Saul. Saul initially looks upon David with love, as David serves him by playing the lyre to ward off the evil spirits which torment Saul. Then Saul asks Jesse specifically for permission to have David stay at the palace and be his armourbearer. David is best friends with Saul's son and marries his daughter – in theory, this could have been a beautiful relationship of mentorship and even succession planning. But, as is often the case, human nature gets in the way, power corrupts and the ego is allowed to run the show. This is common in so many contexts – organisations, government, churches and even families. How do we guard against it?

We can begin by asking God to help us to look past our need to feel important in order to recognise the causes that are bigger than ourselves. We can remind ourselves that we are part of God's plan and work in the world and not the other way around. We can practise collaboration and making room for the gifts of others where we work, worship and live. We can do our part to support, encourage and bless other women, especially those who are younger than us.

Is there a younger woman you know who would be blessed by your encouragement? Find a way to offer that to her in the next few weeks and commit to praying for her in the meantime.

SELINA STONE

Creativity in crisis

Michal let David down through the window; he fled away and escaped. Michal took an idol and laid it on the bed; she put a net of goats' hair on its head and covered it with the clothes. When Saul sent messengers to take David, she said, 'He is sick.' (NRSV)

Today we will take a moment to consider one of the women caught in the middle of these complex circumstances involving Saul and David. Michal is the daughter of Saul and the wife of David and is linked very closely to these two very strong male protagonists. We do not have a lot of detail about her life (as is often the case with women in the biblical text). Yet in this episode Michal comes to the fore, as a courageous and creative person who saves David's life.

Imagine her life for a moment. As the daughter of the king, she would have had a very significant public role. While she would have had more resources and comforts than the average woman of her time, she would have had no control over her life or her inevitably political marriage. She was very fortunate to end up married to a man she actually loved – but then had to deal with the conflict of him becoming the sworn enemy of her father. However, far from being victimised by these circumstances, she offers a creative solution in this moment of crisis.

As women, we may often find ourselves in scenarios that are beyond our control, in our relationships with bosses, friends, partners, children, in our workplaces or churches. We can often be acted upon by others and weighed down by other people's choices, problems or issues – how often have you cleaned up a mess someone else has made, either literally or figuratively? In this text today, Michal encourages us to remember that we can use our agency and capacity to act (even in small ways) and make a big difference. She reminds us to use our creativity and imagination in subtle ways to ease the strain and make a way of escape. She presents to us the gift of womanhood even in the midst of adversity.

Loving Father, I know that you see the pressurised situations that I am facing. Inspire me with creative solutions and with wisdom to know what to say, what to do and how to bring a change in these circumstances.

SELINA STONE

Faithful friendship

David rose from beside the stone heap and prostrated himself with his face to the ground. He bowed three times, and they kissed each other, and wept with each other; David wept the more. Then Jonathan said to David, 'Go in peace.' (NRSV)

The friendship between David and Jonathan is one of the most moving examples in the scriptures. Here, these two men, who have been through so much together, must separate in order that David might flee and save his life. Jonathan has defied his own father in order to save his friend, who the scriptures say he loved 'more than his own soul'. This relationship can seem out of place in our current society. We very rarely see intimate friendships between men being promoted. Instead, in our over-sexualised culture, any intimacy is assumed to be sexual and the fear of being misunderstood can make these friendships even more rare.

However, even as women we can forget the importance of deep friendships. While at one stage of life friendships with other women might be central, at other times when life shifts and changes, connections can be lost. This can be a normal and healthy process, but it may be a sign that we have neglected those gifts God has given to us, in the form of our own personal sisterhood. Having women to share the journey with is crucial to our flourishing – whether or not you have a spouse. We all need friends with whom we can share our burdens and joys, laugh and cry, take trips or go for drinks. David and Jonathan make a covenant of friendship so deep that they bring their descendants into the equation. This is unimaginable in our transient culture, but how might we commit to make deep connections with our friends and those God has gifted to us at this stage in our journey?

Find time this week to reconnect with a friend you appreciate and arrange to visit them, meet for a coffee or do something even more fun that you can enjoy together.

SELINA STONE

Cave formation

David left there and escaped to the cave of Adullam… Everyone who was in distress, and everyone who was in debt, and everyone who was discontented gathered to him; and he became captain over them. Those who were with him numbered about four hundred. (NRSV)

I am not sure if you have ever had to 'pick a team'. I remember not being very sporty at school and often being picked towards the end for netball or rounders. If we have the choice of who we work with or partner with, it is human nature to try to involve the 'best' people to make sure you win. However, this group of people David is leading are far from what we might imagine when we consider a 'dream team': they are suffering in terms of mental health, have no resources and are emotionally unsettled. But David does not reject them. He was used to working within a very well-structured military operation with trained soldiers and equipment. Suddenly, he now finds himself hiding in a cave and leading a motley crew.

David shows us what consistency looks like in a person's character, regardless of the circumstances. He teaches us to be present with those who are suffering and marginalised in the world rather than seeing them as inferior. David's own distress has led him to this cave, a place he did not even know existed while he was enjoying life in the palace, but these men have been suffering all along. This will change him forever.

Sometimes we can find ourselves in a kind of cave through the pain we suffer in life. Life can seem great, and then suddenly we find ourselves in distress and in need of a place of refuge. It is in these moments that we learn compassion as we identify with the pain that others also experience. While the cave can be wet and dark and gloomy, it is a space where God will shape and mould us even more into his image.

Can you remember a time of distress and pain in your own experience? Who was present with you during that time? How did that season shape and change you for the good?

SELINA STONE

Wisdom listens

David said to Abigail… 'Blessed is your advice and blessed are you…' David received from her hand what she had brought him, and said to her, 'Go up in peace to your house. See, I have heeded your voice and respected your person.' (NKJV)

This is one of my favourite stories in the life of David. If wisdom is knowing what to do in a given moment, then Abigail is the embodiment of wisdom. Burdened with an evil, ego-driven husband with a harsh tongue, she manages to manoeuvre around him to save not only her own life but her entire town. In the end she becomes David's wife, which is not a bad conclusion in her case.

However, this story also reflects very well on David, who is able to put his pride aside and listen to the wisdom of Abigail even in the heat of conflict. This is not an easy decision to make; even those with the best intentions will often tend to respond very strongly before pausing to hear alternative perspectives. David accepts her advice, declaring that he has 'heeded' her voice and 'respected' her person. It is often true that listening and respect go hand in hand. We tend listen very deeply to those who we admire or consider to be knowledgeable and sensible. It can feel demeaning and even insulting when we speak and someone talks over us or is doing something else while we talk. David takes in every word she says, even though he had decided on a course of action, and in doing so avoids violence.

In our own families, workplaces, churches and friendships, listening to others and having our voices heard can be difficult. Maybe there are many people clamouring for attention at once; maybe we do not agree with what someone else is saying, or others reject what we have to say. It takes humility and patience to communicate well, a willingness to pause our internal narratives and open up to the wisdom someone may have to offer us.

Is there a person you have had tension or conflict with in your family, church, workplace or social circle? Practise deep listening next time you have a conversation and see how you might grow in understanding and wisdom.

SELINA STONE

A time to mourn

Then David took hold of his clothes and tore them; and all the men who were with him did the same. They mourned and wept, and fasted until evening for Saul and for his son Jonathan, and for the army of the Lord and for the house of Israel. (NRSV)

Grief comes up time and time again in the Bible, as we follow the births, lives and deaths of God's people. On this occasion, grief is complicated for David. He has lost his dear brother-friend Jonathan on the battlefield, whom he loved as his own soul and who saved his life. This is surely an almost indescribable pain for him. But Saul has also died, and alongside the grief for this man whom David respected and served in times gone by, there must also be a sense of relief. David had been on the run from Saul, who had lost all sense of perspective and had tried to take David's life many times, but from this moment, David no longer has to fear that threat.

It can be difficult in our time and culture to know what to do with grief. I know I experienced this when I lost my mom a couple of years ago. In our happy, joyful church singing, upbeat sermons and cheerful greetings – what do we do with lament, grief and loss? Some choose to hide it, mustering up a smile and a 'fine, thank you' when asked how they are; others withdraw, unable to keep up with the expectation to always be positive because that's what God wants…right? I love that David and his men do not hold back but fully express their pain and grief and all the other emotions mixed in. In the Psalms we read so many passages where writers honestly pour out their emotions and feelings. God welcomes and wants the truth from us. After all, no intimate relationship can be built on pretence.

Read Psalm 44 and, in your prayers, speak honestly to God about any feelings of grief, loss, disappointment or sadness you may have. Trust that he knows and loves you, and ask him to intervene.

SELINA STONE

Hospitality and justice

David said to him, 'Do not be afraid, for I will show you kindness for the sake of your father Jonathan; I will restore to you all the land of your grandfather Saul, and you yourself shall eat at my table always.' (NRSV)

In this story, David shows us what restoration and justice look like in a real and tangible way. Mephibosheth is physically disabled because his nurse dropped him as a young child when she heard the news that Saul and Jonathan had died. He has suffered in more ways than most because of that trauma. In the light of all that has happened to Saul and Jonathan, David searches for a descendant he can bless and chooses this son of his brother-friend Jonathan. He does not simply give him back his ancestral lands so that he might have his wealth restored, but he also invites him to eat at his table like one of the king's own sons.

There is a lot of talk about justice nowadays, especially social justice, in the context of our Christian faith. We can often focus on charity – giving donations and short-term assistance to individuals in need, which has the added bonus of making us feel good about ourselves. But 'acts of justice' are the much more costly response to the needs of the poor, marginalised and vulnerable. True biblical justice demands that we are willing to pay a price, to give up our privilege and to make room at the table for those who have been excluded. Charity can be done at arm's length, but justice demands proximity.

This table reminds me of the Lord's table – a table at which none of us deserve to have a seat, but to which through the justice of God we have been welcomed. He did not keep us far away but drew us close, that we might also give a seat to our neighbours and even our enemies.

Dear Lord, thank you for the hospitality that you showed to us in loving us when we were yet sinners. Help me to extend hospitality and commit to acts of justice for those around me who are in need.

SELINA STONE

Sin, sex and power

David sent and enquired about the woman. And one said, 'Is not this Bathsheba, the daughter of Eliam, the wife of Uriah the Hittite?' So David sent messengers and took her, and she came to him, and he lay with her... And the woman conceived. (ESV)

This episode of lust and murder on the part of David is probably the lowest moment of his life as king. At home when his soldiers are out on duty, he takes advantage of his position as king and has sex with Bathsheba, who is married to Uriah. (She would have had no choice in the matter, just to be clear.) David resorts to setting up Uriah to be killed in the same way Saul tried to have him killed. It is a messy story, where lust and power collide and bring out the worst in David, this man chosen from the fields, who killed Goliath and is known as 'a man after God's heart'.

The kindness of God is seen in the fact that he sends the prophet Nathan to convict and challenge David rather than allowing him to fall deeper into the hole he has made. David responds as he should, admitting his guilt and repenting. We can on occasion find ourselves in very deep holes of our own making. It is so easy for us to be carried away with our feelings and needs, especially when it comes to our sexual desires, which can be overwhelming. This story helps us to see the good boundaries that are necessary for us to enjoy and fulfil those needs in ways that do not harm others and ourselves. We must be those who respect the covenants and commitments we have made and those others have made. Where we make mistakes, we should be quick to admit them, rather than attempting to cover our tracks and inevitably making them worse. Our God is kind and quick to forgive and help us back on the right track.

Our sensuality and sexuality are gifts from God which help us to enjoy being alive. How might you embrace and boundary these aspects of your humanity in ways which enhance your life?

SELINA STONE

Blind spots

Absalom commanded his servants, 'Mark when Amnon's heart is merry with wine, and when I say to you, 'Strike Amnon', then kill him. Do not fear; have I not commanded you? Be courageous and be valiant.' So the servants of Absalom did to Amnon as Absalom had commanded. (ESV)

Absalom commits an act of revenge here, after two years of waiting, because Amnon raped his sister Tamar and David did nothing about it. We know that David is said to have been angry, but while Tamar spends the rest of her life destitute in Absalom's house, life goes on as normal for Amnon – that is, until this moment. Women were not recognised as very significant in these times, but it seems particularly negligent for David to take no action. His unwillingness to reprimand his firstborn son results in Absalom taking justice into his own hands.

It is a very human thing to have blind spots, and we have already seen some of David's. It seems that while David might manage his kingdom relatively well, he struggles to be attentive to his internal, personal and family life. It may seem that this problem is not too serious – but time and time again we see that the personal affects the public. David's entire kingdom is at risk later on because he did not handle his family conflicts.

This failure of integration is a very common problem today – we often believe the lie that we can separate our lives into compartments. We can spend all our time perfecting our public image (often through social media) while the inner self is crumbling through neglect. God has good desires for our life in its entirety, not just for a section. He is not only interested in your work, calling or vocation, but in your health and well-being, your relationships and your enjoyment of life. Where there are issues that are not dealt with, he wants to shine a light – not to expose you, but to address them and put things right so that you may flourish alongside those you love.

Loving Father, you are able to see all the hidden places of my life and you love me without condition. Help me to see those aspects of my life which are neglected and in need of your light.

SELINA STONE

The 'never-leaving' God

The Lord is a stronghold for the oppressed, a stronghold in times of trouble. And those who know your name put their trust in you, for you, O Lord, have not forsaken those who seek you. (ESV)

We have traced through a roller coaster of events and situations from the lives of Saul, Jonathan and David. We end today, with a psalm written by David which captures what he has known of God in the midst of all of his difficult times. He has been a shepherd in the field, fought giants and won, been on the run for his life, taken advantage of others, killed many people, been full of grief and despair; but also experienced great joy and happiness. His conclusion through all of these things is that God is where you can be safe when life is hard, and he never leaves those who are looking for his help.

It can be difficult to hold on to these words at times – we can be weighed down by fear and insecurity like Saul was, feel totally unable to handle what life has thrown our way just like David, and be forced to make heartbreaking decisions like Jonathan. But we are those who know the name of God and can decide each day to put our trust in God. We can look back at the testimonies of those who have gone before to see that God is very good at staying with us, and even when we may feel far away, he has never moved.

As you read through this psalm, think and recall the wonderful deeds of God. Perhaps you could write down about those fears you have today, where you feel overwhelmed, unsure and afraid. Write next to them the words of the psalm that are relevant and remind yourself that the God who called and kept David is the same one who hears your prayers and guards your steps.

Think about those people around you are feel oppressed or are in times of trouble. Pray for them today. Ask God to meet with them and to let them know his presence.

SELINA STONE

Knowing Jesus: letter to the Colossians

Deborah Humphries writes:

I wonder how you feel about the idea of studying Colossians. Is it a book you know well or one that you're looking forward to exploring? Maybe you studied it during Bible Month 2019, which focused on Colossians.

Colossians is one of those books that can be read in one sitting in terms of length, but it's also one that is so rich in terms of content that you could spend hours contemplating and digesting each paragraph.

In his letter to the Colossians, Paul warns against false teaching and encourages his readers to know for themselves the fullness of Christ.

With Advent looming, perhaps your mind is full of to-do lists – presents to buy, cards to write, parcels to send, cooking to be done. Perhaps there are play costumes to find or make, performances to attend. Or maybe the house is quiet, and you don't understand what all the fuss is about.

At a time when we are invited to slow down and prepare for the coming of Christ, often our churches, as well as our personal lives, become much busier. In the run-up to Christmas there are many opportunities to share the gospel with those outside the walls of our church. People want to hear about the baby and the young couple, the singing angels, the adoring shepherds and the worshipping magi.

On these occasions I try to share with those eager to hear the Christmas story that Easter is part of that story too. I share the reality of the gospel, explaining how this cute little baby came to live a human life, how he was a refugee, how he experienced joy and friendship, pain, sorrow and betrayal, how he came to die that we might live. I tell people that knowing Jesus is as real today in the ups and downs of life, as it was in first-century Palestine.

Whether you approach Advent with anxiety or serenity or something in between, I pray that during this next week, as you study the book of Colossians, the Holy Spirit will help you grow in your faith and enable you to know Jesus more fully. I pray that you will have the courage to share with others what knowing Jesus means for you and what it could mean for them.

Knowing and growing

In our prayers for you we always thank God, the Father of our Lord Jesus Christ, for we have heard of your faith in Christ Jesus and of the love that you have for all the saints, because of the hope laid up for you in heaven. (NRSV)

How did you first come to know Jesus? Did you read about him? Did you have a 'Damascus Road experience'? Did you gradually come to realise that knowing Jesus was for you? Or did someone you know talk to you about how they knew Jesus?

I was brought up in a Christian home, taken to church, encouraged to talk about faith and ask questions. As I watched Paul Field's *Daybreak*, a musical telling the Easter story through the words and experiences of the first disciples, I came to understand that knowing Jesus was something I could own for myself. I doubt I would have reached that conclusion without the love, prayers and nurturing of friends, family and church members.

In his opening to the letter to the church in Colossae, Paul acknowledges the part Epaphras, 'beloved fellow-servant' and 'faithful minister of Christ', played in bringing the Colossians to faith. Paul notes how on hearing the gospel they 'truly comprehended the grace of God'. But that was only the beginning. From thereon in, they grew in the knowledge of God and bore fruit, enabling them to 'lead lives worthy of the Lord'.

This growth and fruit-bearing did not just happen on its own. It came about because Paul and others continued to uphold them in prayer, praying for their growth and for their knowledge to increase, for spiritual wisdom, for strength, patience and joy in God's power and by God's grace.

For me, these verses underline the importance of prayer and thanksgiving and of being part of the Christian family. As we pray for one another and encourage one another, so we will grow and bear fruit. We might sometimes need to pray for endurance and patience, but in so doing, we will live lives marked by faith, hope and love.

Think again about those people who have been important in your faith journey. Give thanks for them. Now think about the people you know. Who might God be calling you to nurture? What is your prayer for them?

DEBORAH HUMPHRIES

Knowing Jesus, knowing God

He is the image of the invisible God… For in him all the fullness of God was pleased to dwell, and through him God was pleased to reconcile to himself all things, whether on earth or in heaven, by making peace through the blood of his cross. (NRSV)

This passage says much about Jesus, but it also reminds us that in getting to know Jesus, we come to know God. In the NRSV these verses are headed 'The Supremacy of Christ', signifying that Jesus is above all and over all; undeniably, he is 'the firstborn of all creation' and 'the head of the body, the church'. For some, this might be overwhelming and intimidating, but I draw comfort from the image of Christ as 'the firstborn'. Jesus, God's salvation plan, was there in the beginning, as the world came into being: before I was born, before I knew that God wanted to be in relationship with me.

I might not understand the mystery of the cross, but I do know that in being prepared to die, Jesus wanted me to know him, to know God. Because of this selfless act I have become 'securely established and steadfast in the faith' and I will be able to live in 'the hope promised by the gospel', 'the hope… which has been proclaimed to every creature under heaven'.

I have been a Christian since my late teens, but only in recent years have I come to understand John 3:16 as being about the redemption of all creation. 'For God so loved the world that he gave his only Son.' God loves the world – not just you and me, not just those who know him, but the world and everything in it.

As I have become braver and more convinced of this, I have begun to openly share the gospel, the good news of God's love, with the world. I do this often hesitatingly, sometimes bravely, occasionally easily; but because knowing Jesus is fundamental to my life, to my very being, I cannot help but share my experience with those I meet.

Jesus the firstborn, image of the invisible God, thank you for being there since the world began, thank you for being. Give me the courage to share the gospel, in ways that make sense to those I meet.

DEBORAH HUMPHRIES

Knowing and understanding

I want their hearts to be encouraged and united in love, so that they may have all the riches of assured understanding and have the knowledge of God's mystery, that is, Christ himself, in whom are hidden all the treasures of wisdom and knowledge. (NRSV)

Paul opens this section of his letter with the words, 'I am now rejoicing in my sufferings.' I cannot honestly say I rejoice in my sufferings. In fact, like others, I try to avoid suffering rather than accept it as part of life.

During Holy Week, a small group from our church gathered at the station to greet commuters with hot cross buns and chocolate eggs as a sign of God's love and grace. We were met with suspicion by some, bemusement by others and often a total lack of understanding that we might possibly offer such treats with no expectation of anything in return.

As we waited, my mind turned to the different varieties of 'hot cross bun' in the shops – some filled with sweet, juicy fruit, others with chocolate – seeming to ignore the bitter, original flavourings reminiscent of Christ's death and the anticipated anointing of his body with spices.

In our small, faithful act of witness that Holy Week, we had a few conversations which began to explore the mystery of faith, of Christ's suffering, death and resurrection and of God's unconditional love for all creation. We may not have brought anyone to Christ that day, but my hope is that it might have been one more step towards making 'the word of God fully known' and understanding 'the riches of the glory of this mystery, which is Christ in you, the hope of glory'.

Paul was determined that the recipients of his letter might be 'encouraged and united in love'. His passion for the gospel meant that he wanted others to experience 'the knowledge of God's mystery… Christ [and]… the treasures of wisdom and knowledge'. How passionate are we about sharing our faith and the understanding it brings?

Incarnate God, as Advent nears, keep us open to opportunities to share the mystery of our faith. Give us courage to reveal more than sanitised images of Jesus' nativity, proclaiming too his' suffering, death and resurrection.

DEBORAH HUMPHRIES

Knowing and holding fast

As you therefore have received Christ Jesus the Lord, continue to live your lives in him, rooted and built up in him and established in the faith... See to it that no one takes you captive through philosophy and empty deceit, according to human tradition... and not according to Christ. (NRSV)

This section of Paul's letter to the Corinthians offers us both reassurance and challenge. In knowing Jesus, we are to 'continue to live [our] lives in him, rooted and built up in him and established in the faith'. Sounds easy. Just keep going! But then comes the challenge. We need to hold fast to the teaching of Jesus. We must not be led astray by false teaching. So how exactly do we work out what is of Christ and what is human tradition?

There are many things about which Christians agree, but there are also many examples of where Christian theology differs. How do we avoid a 'human way of thinking' and 'hold... fast to the head'? How can we achieve unity in the body of Christ so that it 'grows with a growth that is from God'?

I think the key lies in the text. It's about being part of the whole body. We cannot go off on our own and decide what is of God and what is not. We need to work out our theology in community with others who know Jesus. Of course, we will still disagree. Some parts of the church will think one thing and other parts of the church will hold an opposing view, each believing that after much prayer, consideration and deliberation, they have the 'right' answer.

We are called to try and remain 'held together'. In some things perhaps we need to find a way of what Methodists call 'living with contradictory convictions'. This might still be painful, but if we can respect one another, listen carefully, be open to the possibility of change and hold fast to the head, then the whole body will continue to be nourished and held together.

Think of an example of where the church lives 'with contradictory convic-tions'. Pray for unity in the body of Christ. Do you need to express your views or listen to others?

DEBORAH HUMPHRIES

Knowing and being raised up

**So if you have been raised with Christ, seek the things that are above…
And be thankful. Let the word of Christ dwell in you richly; teach and
admonish one another in all wisdom; and with gratitude in your hearts
sing psalms, hymns, and spiritual songs to God. (NRSV)**

What do you do when you need 'raising up'? I like to swim and sing,
although not usually both at the same time! When life is difficult, the
physical activity of swimming lengths invigorates me. Often, I use the time
to process or to pray. When I am truly relaxed, I get lost in the rhythm of my
stroke, the sound of the water and the beauty of the sky outside.

One morning, my swim was transformed by a woman singing the hymn
'You raise me up'. Instead of being bored by her repetition of the same few
lines, I was reminded of these words from Colossians: 'With gratitude in
your hearts sing psalms, hymns, and spiritual songs to God.' This woman's
infectious joy reminded me that I have already been 'raised with Christ',
and I wanted to respond by praising God in song.

We are already raised with Christ, and yet we must still strive to 'put to
death… whatever in [us] is earthly'. I love that image of stripping off the
old stuff and clothing ourselves with the new. Just like we might sneak
back our favourite comfortable jumper out of the bin, we sometimes slip
back into our old ways. The writer of Colossians recognises this using the
language of 'being renewed'.

Dying to the old self is not immediate and permanent, it is a process,
but it is helped by allowing 'the word of Christ [to] dwell in' us. If we clothe
ourselves 'with compassion, kindness, humility, meekness, and patience';
if we 'bear with one another… forgive each other… clothe [ourselves] with
love' ,then we will find ourselves raised up, filled with gratitude, singing
psalms, hymns, and spiritual songs to God.

---

*As we get to know Jesus, we will become more like him. What words need to
dwell in us to enable this to happen? What songs will we sing (metaphorically
or otherwise) in gratitude to God?*

DEBORAH HUMPHRIES

Knowing and relating

Wives, be subject to your husbands, as is fitting in the Lord. Husbands, love your wives and never treat them harshly. Children, obey your parents in everything, for this is your acceptable duty in the Lord. Fathers, do not provoke your children, or they may lose heart. (NRSV)

Some of Paul's writing seems at odds with present-day thinking about equality. Perhaps there is something more profound beneath a literal interpretation of Paul's words. This passage could be interpreted as extolling the merits of relationships built on mutual respect and trust, where each member of the (biological or church) family wants the best for the other and each has something to learn from the other.

One wet day, I drove past a woman playing with two toddlers. The children were splashing in a puddle and poking a stick in the water. It was wet, but they seemed to have plenty of time to play and explore the world around them. Maybe these children had enabled the older woman to see the puddle with fresh eyes, a source of pleasure rather than something to be avoided.

Families come in all shapes and sizes, but the strongest families are built on mutual loving relationships where each is respected whatever age or stage of life they are at. Sometimes children learn from adults; sometimes adults learn from children.

For Christians, the perfect relationship is seen within the Trinity. This equal yet complementary relationship is beautiful, even if it remains something of a mystery. Those of us who know Jesus are invited to join the Godhead, to enter into relationship with Father, Son and Holy Spirit.

Later in this passage Paul addresses slaves, advising them, 'Whatever your task, put yourselves into it, as done for the Lord.' While slavery of any kind or the oppression of any human being are unacceptable, if we can model all our relationships on the relationship we enjoy with the Trinity, we will begin to experience the love and joy that only God can bring.

Relational, three-in-one God, help us to build relationships characterised by love and respect so that others might catch a glimpse of Jesus and come to know you for themselves.

DEBORAH HUMPHRIES

Knowing and being

**Devote yourselves to prayer, keeping alert in it with thanksgiving…
Conduct yourselves wisely towards outsiders, making the most of the
time. Let your speech always be gracious, seasoned with salt, so that
you may know how you ought to answer everyone. (NRSV)**

It was one of those days… A rare lie-in was cut short by responding to the
needs of my distressed daughter; my phone revealed a text cancelling a
long-awaited catch-up with a friend… I decided to visit the shops and pay
a cheque in at the bank. The shop I needed was not yet open and the bank
was closed for refurbishment.

I could have easily burst into tears – and, to be fair, as I approach the
menopause, that is often my reaction to things. I decided to 'make the
most of my time', not by stomping home to continue with the unending
list of household chores, but by taking time to just 'be' over a large mug of
coffee. I drafted a reassuring text to my friend and prayed for my daughter's
well-being. For some reason that morning, I had been able to keep my
cool and grab the opportunity to live in the present moment. I had been
thankful, wise and gracious.

Of course, I'm not always like that. There are days when I do not act
wisely, when things get on top of me and life seems unfair and unkind; but
I do try because I want to be the best person I can be.

Paul tells us that living wisely and graciously is not just for our benefit
or even for our nearest and dearest. It's about seizing every opportunity
'to answer everyone', so that if a door is opened, we are ready to 'declare
the mystery of Christ'.

If I had been grumpy that morning in the coffee shop, I might have
missed the opportunity to share the grace of God with the barista, to speak
with her in a way that was 'seasoned with salt', in friendly, health-giving
conversation.

---

*'Be still, and know that I am God' (Psalm 46). Gracious God, give us strength
and patience when life is tough. Help us to make the most of our time and
realise that 'being' is sometimes better than 'doing'.*

DEBORAH HUMPHRIES

The heart

Helen Williams writes:

It's Advent Sunday and a joy to join you as we turn our thoughts towards Christmas, with both excitement and, no doubt, some apprehension at all we hope to achieve before Christmas Day arrives. Incidentally, the best piece of pre-Christmas advice I was ever given was: 'Aim to bless not to impress!'

Traditionally, Advent is a season of preparation, repentance and contemplation – not only of the incomprehensible miracle of 'God with us' in the incarnation, but also of Jesus' second coming in glory. Soon, in carol services across the land, we will be encouraging one another with the words, 'Let every heart prepare him room.' We'll be remembering that God 'imparts to human hearts the blessings of his heaven' and even praying, 'O, come to my heart, Lord Jesus, there is room in my heart for thee.'

Thinking about the words of these carols, I started to wonder what we mean by the word 'heart' and if there were ways we might prepare our hearts more effectively to greet Jesus on Christmas morning. Delving into the Bible, I found around 1,000 references to the heart and began to discover that it can mean so many things: the physical organ (beating over 2.5 billion times in the average lifetime); the place of intellectual activity; the seat of emotions; the centre of the will and of choice; and even a thing inherently evil and in desperate need of regeneration.

The key command God gave his people was to 'love the Lord your God with all your heart and with all your soul and with all your strength' (Deuteronomy 6:5) and, of course, the gospels record Jesus reiterating this, the 'greatest' commandment.

What does it mean to love God with all our heart? What is God's heart like? Why does the writer of Proverbs urge us to guard our heart? How can we be pure in heart? Is your heart one of flesh or stone? Who is this God who not only searches our heart but is close to the broken-hearted?

We know that David was a man 'after God's heart' – what an accolade! Over this fortnight, will you ask God what is on his heart for you and whether there are ways in which he might renew your heart? I know that Jesus asks us, as he did of Bartimaeus, 'What do you want me to do for you?'

'Awake, dear heart, awake'

The hour has already come for you to wake up from your slumber, because our salvation is nearer now than when we first believed. The night is nearly over; the day is almost here. So let us put aside the deeds of darkness and put on the armour of light. (NIV)

It's Advent Sunday and today in many churches the exhortation will be to 'wake up!'.

Wake up, like the woman in Song of Songs whose heart, even as she sleeps, is intently aware of the imminent arrival of the Beloved: 'My heart was awake,' she cries (Song of Songs 5:2). Wake up, those of us living in the dust, says Isaiah, 'shout for joy' and feel the freshness of the morning dew (Isaiah 26:19). 'Wake up, sleeper, rise from the dead,' Paul exhorts the Ephesians (5:14). 'Wake up,' writes John to the church in Sardis (Revelation 3:2), repent and be ready for the returning Lord, who will come as unexpectedly as a thief.

'Wake up from your slumber,' Paul writes again in our reading for today, and 'put on the armour of light' ready for the coming day of the Lord. This time he's writing to the Roman Christians, for whom the hope of the Lord's return must have been deeply reassuring as they faced persecution.

I'm more of a night owl than a morning lark, but Paul exhorts his readers to leap from their beds and put on two things: first, the armour of light, and second, the Lord Jesus Christ himself. That's it! Ask forgiveness for the clinging sins he lists, cast them off and put on Jesus instead. Then you'll be ready, as 'children of the light' (Ephesians 5:8), to live for him, meet him in the baby at Bethlehem and be ready for his return.

We wear him on the outside, and Paul will go on to pray for the Ephesians (3:17) that Christ would 'dwell in [their] hearts' – on the inside too (the Greek word for 'dwell' has the sense of 'stay forever'). Both inside and out, the secret is to be, and to stay, full of Jesus.

As this Advent begins, ask God to search your heart, to forgive and to cleanse you. Then pray for Jesus to fill you to the core, even as you buckle on the 'armour of light' he has ready for you.

HELEN WILLIAMS

A heart condition

Keep [my words] within your heart; for they are life to those who find them and health to one's whole body. Above all else, guard your heart, for everything you do flows from it. (NIV)

I recently had to take my mother for tests on her heart. Although she is pretty well and active for her age, heart disease was diagnosed and she will go on being monitored. This reminded me how important testing and monitoring our metaphorical heart is too, as its condition is so affected by how we live and what we take into it. 'Guard your heart,' says the writer of Proverbs, 'for it determines the course of your life' (v. 23, NLT).

The Hebrew Old Testament writers knew the heart was an organ inside the chest (Nabal's heart attack is described in 1 Samuel 25:37), but they used the word 'heart' for knowing, understanding, having wisdom, discerning between good and evil, feeling emotions, making choices and thinking. This is partly because they had no concept of the brain. Their word *lev* (heart) is actually made up of letters depicting a staff, to demonstrate authority or will, and a home (actually the floor plan of a nomadic tent), so the word literally means 'the home of the will' or 'the authority within'.

We need to check this place of internal authority regularly, as wounds, temptations and disappointment can lead to hurt, ungodly preoccupations and resentment taking root. Working constantly with the Holy Spirit to monitor our heart, even when we don't feel like it, is a real spiritual discipline. 'When you are on your beds, search your hearts and be silent,' says David (Psalm 4:4), and he promises this will lead to sleeping peacefully. In Psalm 139 he prays, 'Search me, God, and know my heart; test me and know my anxious thoughts. See if there is any offensive way in me and lead me in the way everlasting.' He knew the value of keeping short accounts with God and thus preventing heart disease.

On this day in AD60 Jesus' disciple, Andrew, was crucified for his faith. As we ask God to search our hearts today, we thank God for those so serious about their hearts belonging to Jesus they face persecution and death.

HELEN WILLIAMS

The heart of the matter

I will give them singleness of heart and action… I will make an ever-lasting covenant with them: I will never stop doing good to them… I will rejoice in doing them good and will assuredly plant them in this land with all my heart and soul. (NIV)

Today, there will be great excitement in many households as the first door of the Advent calendar is opened. Although many doors will reveal only a chocolate, toy, beauty product or tiny bottle of gin, we know the opening of these doors begins the countdown to the celebration of the most significant revelation the world has ever known: God revealed in human form.

What is the heart of God like, that he should have devised this incredible plan to save us? We see something of it in his conversation with Solomon as the building of the temple reaches completion. God promises that his 'eyes and [his] heart will always be there'. He also promises security for Solomon's kingship if he walks 'faithfully with integrity of heart' (1 Kings 9:3–4). There is a heart-to-heart exchange here: you stay faithful and I will always stay with you.

God's heart of love for his 'beloved' is threaded through the Old Testament but today we look at God's promise to his people through Jeremiah. In Jeremiah 3:15, God had promised 'shepherds after my own heart, who will lead you with knowledge and understanding'. In chapter 31, God talked of yearning for his children and having compassion on them, and here, in chapter 32, he promises, 'I will never stop doing good to them… I will rejoice in doing them good and will assuredly plant them in this land with all my heart and soul.' As in his exchange with Solomon, God wants a reciprocal relationship or covenant with his people, promising to give them singleness of heart and action so they will stay faithful.

God's commitment to his children is unequivocal. His heart is full of goodness, love and compassion, but relationship with him means our heart must reflect his.

George MacDonald, the 19th-century author who much influenced C.S. Lewis, wrote that 'there is a place in God's heart that only you can fill'. It rather turns things upside down to think what we might mean to God!

HELEN WILLIAMS

So dear to my heart

The Sovereign Lord comes with power, and he rules with a mighty arm. See, his reward is with him, and his recompense accompanies him. He tends his flock like a shepherd: he gathers the lambs in his arms and carries them close to his heart. (NIV)

I wonder if you'll hear a performance of Handel's 'Messiah' this season. It's often performed by local choirs in Advent. After its gorgeous opening *sinfony*, the first vocal piece of the whole work presents God's words to his people in Isaiah 40: 'Comfort ye, my people' (not 'Come for tea', as we naughtily used to sing as children!). Here is God's promise of salvation.

Yesterday we looked at God's heart as expressed in Jeremiah's prophecy. Isaiah's prophecy reveals even more. Incidentally, chapter 40 opens the second part of the book of Isaiah, in which references to a different time period indicate that it may well have been written by an exile, some 150 years after Isaiah's death – someone who studied Isaiah's work intently. This would mean that both yesterday and today's passages were written quite close together in time.

In this amazing chapter, often read in Advent because of its prophecy of John the Baptist, God speaks to his people of comfort. The Hebrew word here has overtones of 'fortitude' rather than a fluffy kind of comfort. The Bayeux tapestry shows William the Conqueror prodding his soldiers into battle with a spear. The caption, 'King William comforteth his soldiers', might make us laugh, but there is here too the sense of being roused from lethargy. 'Speak tenderly' literally means 'to speak to the heart' and is a phrase often found in the Bible referring to reassurance or winning someone back. Centuries before Jesus is born, God is promising salvation.

Poignantly, the power, majesty and triumph of our sovereign God in verse 10 is immediately followed by the moving description of that same God who 'tends his flock like a shepherd', gently leading the young mothers and gathering up the lambs and holding them 'close to his heart'. What heartbreaking tenderness!

If you are able to, just sit with God and feel yourself 'close to his heart' for a while. You might also look on to verse 29 for the key to living well in this season!

HELEN WILLIAMS

'I know you by heart'

The Spirit of the Sovereign Lord is on me, because the Lord has anointed me to proclaim good news to the poor. He has sent me to bind up the broken-hearted. (NIV)

Our title today is a line spoken by Sara, the *Little Princess* of Francis Hodgson Burnett's book, to her father who is often away abroad. 'I know you by heart,' she says, 'you are inside my heart.'

Yesterday we were reminded that God carries us 'close to his heart', and today we move to Isaiah 61, to the ancient prophecy fulfilled in Jesus as he reads it in the synagogue in Nazareth at the beginning of his public ministry (Luke 4:16–21). In reading this 'manifesto', Jesus presents the central themes of that ministry to come, and there it is, the second statement he reads: 'He has sent me to 'bind up the broken-hearted.' This echoes Psalm 34:18, where God promises to be 'close to the broken-hearted', and Psalm 147:3 too: 'He heals the broken-hearted and binds up their wounds.'

Our heart-wounds may be inflicted by the carelessness of others or by wrong expectations of ours. Sometimes, we just let our ego or 'false self' take over and there is a sense in the Hebrew here of God saving us from the ravages of our own unbridled ego. How vital it is to find our true self in the presence of our heavenly Father.

Many of us have become aware of a recent resurgence in the ancient Japanese art of *kintsugi* – literally 'golden joinery'. Broken ceramics are mended using resin containing real gold, so that the reformed object reveals a new shining beauty. I once hated it when a wise older lady told me that there was 'beauty in brokenness', but I know that, as we take our broken selves to Jesus and ask him to mend us, reform us and renew us, enabling us to be more fully the person God made us to be, a new beauty develops in us.

Perhaps you might find some pictures of kintsugi today and, as you sit with them, ask God to pour his gold resin into the cracks in your heart, to bind up and mend your heart wherever it is broken.

HELEN WILLIAMS

Love hearts

I pray that out of his glorious riches he may strengthen you with power through his Spirit in your inner being, so that Christ may dwell in your hearts through faith. (NIV)

We thought yesterday about Jesus' compassion for the broken-hearted. What else do the gospels tell us about Jesus' heart? 'I am gentle and humble in heart,' he says to a Galilean crowd, 'come to me' and 'find rest for your souls' (Matthew 11:28–29). In Luke's gospel, we're given another insight when Jesus encounters a widow whose only son has just died: 'His heart went out to her and he said, "Don't cry"' (Luke 7:13). We even find Jesus in John 5:42 accusing the Jewish leaders of not having 'the love of God in [their] hearts'! It's clear that, if we're to be like Jesus, our daily prayer needs to be for our hearts to be characterised by love, compassion, gentleness and humility.

Being consistently loving and compassionate like Jesus is often only part of the challenge for us. Do you ever feel that the sheer number of people you carry in your heart makes this so difficult – perhaps especially at this time of year when thoughts may be turning towards Christmas plans? This season we'll also take many more into our hearts, as Christmas appeals make us aware of so many people who are living in desperate need and real danger.

This community in our heart, ever increasing in size if you're engaged with social media too, can be utterly overwhelming. How do we love and show compassion to so many without burning out? Our passage offers the only solution for our heart: may Christ dwell (the Hebrew word has the sense of being completely at home) in our hearts. As his love takes root in us, we'll begin to understand something of the dimensions of God's love for us and be overwhelmed by him. It's no coincidence that this prayer comes immediately before Paul's teaching on how to love others!

'As we follow his gaze, we find our boundaries constantly shifting. This is the dynamic of being shaped by being overwhelmed,' says David Ford in The Shape of Living (Canterbury Press, 2012). May you be overwhelmed by God.
HELEN WILLIAMS

Cardiac arrest

The Lord your God will circumcise your hearts and the hearts of your descendants, so that you may love him with all your heart and with all your soul, and live. (NIV)

Billy Bray, a Cornish tin miner and 'the companion of drunkards, and… very near hell', had a terrible mining accident in 1823. The story of his heart-warming encounter with God, one November morning, is inspiring. Falling to his knees and crying to God for forgiveness, he was radically transformed, becoming an exuberant preacher around Cornwall, perhaps best known for his cry, 'If they were to put me in a barrel, I would shout "glory!" out through the bunghole!' If we let ourselves be overwhelmed by God's love, as we considered yesterday, this will often result in a longing to be right with God. Revival is always characterised by repentant hearts.

Jesus leaves us in no doubt of the evil the human heart is capable of. You can see his list in Mark 7:20–23, but it is to the Old Testament that we go today, to Moses' final speech to the Israelites (following the ancient pattern of a covenant renewal) as he begs them to return to God and stay faithful. The word 'heart' is mentioned eight times in this chapter alone, and the sense here is very much of the inner self or the will. God is serious about sincere commitment in our deepest places.

Firstly, Moses reminds the people to take to heart the blessings and curses God has provided. Twice he exhorts them to return to God and 'obey him with all your heart'. He even goes so far as to say that God will 'circumcise' their hearts – a visceral metaphor indicating how serious God is about his covenant. This is 'not too difficult for you,' he chides, because God's word is already 'in your heart', but he warns that if their 'heart turns away' then the beautiful covenant will be broken.

You might find it useful to pray Psalm 51, perhaps out loud, today as a prayer of repentance. If you have access to such things, you could listen to the heart-stopping version of it by the composer Allegri ('Miserere').

HELEN WILLIAMS

Pure in heart

We also glory in our sufferings, because we know that suffering produces perseverance; perseverance, character; and character, hope. And hope does not put us to shame, because God's love has been poured out into our hearts through the Holy Spirit, who has been given to us. (NIV)

Yesterday we confessed (together with Moses and David) the tendency of our heart to forget former blessings, to drift into disobedience and to arrogantly choose its own way. The Anglican Church, in which my husband and I work, has a prayer set for today, this second Sunday in Advent, which you can see below. It begins: 'Almighty God, purify our hearts and minds.' It's this idea of developing a pure heart that we'll look at more closely today.

Jesus, in the beatitudes, makes special mention of those who are 'pure in heart', promising that their reward will be 'to see God' (Matthew 5:8). While mentioned in several psalms, in Psalm 73 there is an illuminating study of what it means to *not* be pure in heart! It's worth looking at.

In some ways, being 'pure' doesn't sound much fun. Perhaps our word has overtones of the puritanical abhorrence of things that were fancy, decorated or entertaining. Maybe it just sounds unachievable. The Greek word for 'pure' is *katharos* meaning clean like washed clothes, sifted like wheat or unadulterated like metal without any alloy. In other words, we're blessed if our motives are unmixed and true.

God gives us the ability to be authentic and real with him as we seek to be more like Jesus.

Of course, there's no way we can be pure of heart by our own efforts, and Romans 5 has the key in verse 5: it is the Holy Spirit, literally 'poured out into our hearts' who effects the changes – cleaning, nudging, convicting, enabling, empowering and replacing dross with God's love.

Almighty God, purify our hearts and minds, that when your Son Jesus Christ comes again as Judge and Saviour, we may be ready to receive him, who is our Lord and our God. Amen

HELEN WILLIAMS

My resting heart rate

Let the peace of Christ rule in your hearts… And be thankful. Let the message of Christ dwell among you richly as you teach and admonish one another with all wisdom through psalms, hymns, and songs from the Spirit, singing to God with gratitude in your hearts. (NIV)

As we let God's Holy Spirit purify our heart, it follows that there will be a stillness in that deep place at our centre. 'You have made us for yourself and our hearts are restless until they find their rest in you,' wrote St Augustine in his *Confessions*. I'm sure you have known times of being completely at peace with God, 'calmed and quietened', as Psalm 131:2 says, with 'breathing room for your soul (Psalm 62:2, MSG).

1 Peter 3:4 also challenges us to let our 'adorning' be 'the hidden person of the heart with the imperishable beauty of a gentle and quiet spirit, which in God's sight is very precious' (ESV). A woman whose heart is at rest and fully present is able to invite others to rest and be themselves, to let go of striving and restlessness – to enter into God's heart. In his book, *The Way of the Heart*, Henri Nouwen describes Anthony of the Desert, who spent years in solitude seeking God. When he came out of the desert, Nouwen writes, 'somehow his solitude had become an infinite space into which anyone could be invited'. I do a lot of travelling around with my husband in his role as a bishop, and a wise friend recently challenged me to be like a 'tabernacle' (the portable, earthly dwelling place of God for the Israelites) wherever I go – taking a space in which people can meet Jesus. That's quite a challenge, but it's going to be my prayer.

The key to the quiet heart, as Paul writes to the Colossians, is to let Christ's peace 'rule' our hearts. There are three vital things: inviting the prince of peace to capture your heart, allowing God's word to permeate it and living a life of gratitude.

It's 18 days until Christmas. Could you find time to seek solitude in God's presence today?

HELEN WILLIAMS

A tuned heart

Good friend, take to heart what I'm telling you; collect my counsels and guard them with your life. Tune your ears to the world of Wisdom; set your heart on a life of Understanding. (MSG)

A heart at rest in God can receive and assimilate his wisdom. I'm reminded of a phrase from John Donne's poem, written when contemplating his death: 'I tune the instrument at the door.' Oh, for a heart in tune with the heart of God! I work as an accompanist, and the first thing I do with any instrumentalist is to ensure their instrument is in tune with my piano – not always easy when it's a beginner – or else an unharmonious and jarring performance ensues!

The writer of this discourse urges the reader to tune their ears to wisdom, understanding and knowledge. Solomon takes up this theme in 23:12: 'Apply your heart to instruction and your ears to words of knowledge,' he writes (NIV). Learning to listen to and recognise God's voice and align our will with his is vital. David encourages us to do this even while we sleep, 'I will praise the Lord, who counsels me; even at night my heart instructs me' (Psalm 16:7, NIV).

Sometimes, as we pray, God gives us a word for someone. The wise lady who taught me about brokenness (see 3 December) also advised me that a large proportion of what the Holy Spirit may show us will be to fuel our prayers for others, not to share directly. I've found this helpful advice – there are times when it's more sensitive to pray rather than tell people what you think God is saying to them.

Proverbs 20:5 provides great advice on helping others: 'The purposes of a person's heart are deep waters, but one who has insight draws them out' (NIV). 'Drawing out' another's heart can be a gift to them, but, as the next verse warns, If you're going to help someone articulate what's on their heart, you'd better be 'faithful' to them.

Let's pray today that God will teach us to tune into a sense of eternity – his big picture and plan for us and for our world.

HELEN WILLIAMS

King of hearts

'You know him, for he lives with you and will be in you. I will not leave you as orphans; I will come to you… Anyone who loves me will obey my teaching. My Father will love them, and we will come to them and make our home with them.' (NIV)

An ancient story tells of God discussing with his angels where he might hide himself in his creation, so that people would grow through searching for him. All sorts of places are suggested – from the depths of the earth to the moon – until finally an old angel suggests that God hide himself in the depths of people's hearts. 'They'll never think to look there,' he says!

In our reading today, from Jesus' farewell discourses, he promises his disciples (and therefore us), that if we ask, the Holy Spirit will be with us and in us . 'You are in me, and I am in you,' he says (v. 20). He even adds that he and the Father will make their home with us, so begs his disciples not to allow their hearts to be 'troubled'.

I'm often apt to forget that God, in three persons, lives in my inmost being or heart. How awesome that the Holy Spirit, 'who searches our hearts', is there, interceding for us 'in accordance with the will of God' (Romans 8:27). I think if I were properly aware of this miracle, I'd spend more time attempting to tune into what's going on. The 19th-century Russian mystic, Theophan the Recluse, wrote: 'To pray is to descend with the mind into the heart, and there to stand before the face of the Lord, ever-present, all-seeing, within you.' May that be our goal!

There is a wonderful story in Genesis 24 of Abraham's servant, who is tasked with finding a wife for Isaac. Praying 'in his heart', he expects God to work, experiences God's prophetic leading, is watchful for his response and ends up full of gratitude and worship.

We're told twice in Luke 2 of Mary 'pondering' things in her heart. Might there be the opportunity today to ponder a little yourself, quietening your mind and tuning into God in your heart?

HELEN WILLIAMS

An inscribed heart

'This is the covenant I will make with them… I will put my laws in their hearts, and I will write them on their minds'… Let us draw near to God with a sincere heart and with the full assurance that faith brings, having our hearts sprinkled to cleanse us. (NIV)

Having pondered the miracle of God within and the reminder that if we can let go and let God be God all will be well, today we look at what it means to have God's word in our hearts. The writer to the Hebrews quotes Jeremiah with God's promise that he will 'put [his] laws in [our] hearts'. He goes on to describe the 'new and living way' opened up to us through the cross, enabling us to 'draw near to God'. Our hearts thereby 'sprinkled' clean, we may now approach him in 'sincerity of heart'.

It seems a far cry from when the law was first given to the Israelites and they were told to 'fix' God's words in their 'hearts and minds, tie them as symbols on your hands and bind them on your foreheads' (Deuteronomy 11:18–20).

Moses was creative, too, suggesting they attach them to their door frames and gates. For followers of Jesus, his death and resurrection did away with the need for sacrifice and ritual, but sometimes I wonder if we take a great deal for granted. God has written his word into our hearts, but do we really live, eat and breathe it? Are we like a stick of seaside rock with God's words written right through us?

In Psalm 19, David challenges our love for God's word or 'law', describing it as perfect, refreshing, trustworthy, wisdom-inducing, joy-giving, radiant, enlightening, righteous, precious and sweeter than honey! Jesus, of course, is our supreme example: in the wilderness, he combats every intolerable temptation with the words, 'It is written…' and a triumphant scriptural blow to the enemy!

How can we ensure that God's words are ready on our lips when temptation, challenge or the need for wise discernment arises? God already promises his word is in our hearts, but could we do more to internalise it?

HELEN WILLIAMS

Heart transplant

I will give them an undivided heart and put a new spirit in them; I will remove from them their heart of stone and give them a heart of flesh. Then they will follow my decrees and be careful to keep my laws. They will be my people, and I will be their God. (NIV)

Once we allow God to write his word on our heart, his work begins in earnest. It's a graphic picture here: stone – so hard, so cold, so dead – and flesh – so soft, so warm, so alive. A flesh heart is more vulnerable, too, and it can be tempting to turn a cold heart from both God and others, for fear of what they may ask of us. I have a smooth, polished stone heart by my bed, and last week I added to it a rough, heart-shaped stone I found on the beach. They are reminders to me that I need to pray constantly for a heart of flesh.

In chapter 37 Ezekiel describes his vision of the valley of bones. Again, the theme is life where death has reigned. Exiled in Babylon, Ezekiel warns his fellow exiles of their moral failure, but also offers unbelievable hope for the future in God's promise: 'I will make breath enter you, and you will come to life. I will attach tendons to you and make flesh come upon you and cover you with skin; I will put breath in you, and you will come to life' (Ezekiel 37:5–6). Yes, Lord, an 'undivided', living heart, please!

The text messages I send are often punctuated with hearts, beating hearts and faces with heart eyes! I'm good at expressing love for people and things like this, but whether my heart is being daily transformed to be more like God's heart of love is another question. How can we put ourselves in the way of this transformation? I recently heard the advice of Mother Teresa: 'Spend one hour a day in adoration of your Lord and never do anything you know is wrong and you will be alright.'

For some of us, an hour a day in adoration is quite impossible. Five minutes may be all you can manage, but do spend whatever time you can make today adoring your Lord and opening your heart to him.

HELEN WILLIAMS

Take heart!

We do not lose heart. Though outwardly we are wasting away, yet inwardly we are being renewed day by day. For our light and momentary troubles are achieving for us an eternal glory that far outweighs them all. (NIV)

How good it is to hear these encouraging words from Paul, twice in this chapter: 'We do not lose heart.' What's the secret of this good news for our heart? Once again, it is God's initiative: in the beginning he, who is himself light (1 John 1:5), created light (and it was good) and now makes his light shine in our hearts. Light dispels darkness, bringing clarity and growth, but the main purpose of this light is to enable us to actually know 'God's glory displayed in the face of Christ'. As we draw nearer to Christmas, we can have confidence that we will see and know 'God with us' in the baby Jesus.

Paul is also jubilantly confident that, although our bodies are 'jars of clay' and 'wasting away', we are being 'renewed day by day'. Out of his own suffering, Paul offers us future hope and absolute confidence in the eternal glory to come, by comparison with which all problems fade into insignificance.

Three Old Testament kings obviously had God's light in their hearts. 'Neither before nor after Josiah was there a king like him who turned to the Lord as he did – with all his heart' (2 Kings 23:25); Jehoshaphat's 'heart was devoted to the ways of the Lord' (2 Chronicles 17:6); and Asa's 'heart was fully committed to the Lord all his life' (1 Kings 15:14). It's reassuring though that, despite this tribute, Asa had to be pulled up short by a seer and reminded that 'the eyes of the Lord range throughout the earth to strengthen those whose hearts are fully committed to him' (2 Chronicles 16:9). God is all about renewing and strengthening hearts; after all, he is the one 'who forms the hearts of all' (Psalm 33:15).

'In every situation, by prayer and petition, with thanksgiving, present your requests to God. And the peace of God, which transcends all understanding, will guard your hearts and your minds in Christ Jesus' (Philippians 4:6–7).
HELEN WILLIAMS

Things Jesus said: Matthew's gospel

Karin Ling writes:

I still find it amazing that we can read the actual words that came out of Jesus' mouth – what a privilege! We can be taught by his wisdom, disciplined by his perfect love and comforted by his compassion all these years after he lived on earth. His words are alive by the power of the Holy Spirit – 'For the word of God is alive and active' (Hebrews 4:12) – and can change our lives remarkably. Sometimes this change is in small, slow ways over a long period of time and sometimes quite suddenly as we see a startling truth and know we must respond immediately.

Looking at Jesus' words in more detail also helps us get to know him better – to know his character. This will then make us feel closer to him and more easily able to pray to him 'in all things', as the apostle Paul recommends in Ephesians 6:18. It also helps us to hear and recognise his voice speaking to us directly. As it says in John 10:27 (NIV), 'My sheep listen to my voice; I know them, and they follow me.' We must make sure we know Jesus' voice and have faith to obey. Seeing how those around him were blessed and changed by his words gives us confidence in Jesus' authority, so we are more willing to obey him.

The quotations for this week are taken from the middle section of the gospel of Matthew. They begin after his baptism and cover the start of his active ministry. At this time, he spoke not only through the beatitudes and parables but also into people's specific situations as he moved from place to place meeting all kinds of people. He was also explaining things more fully to his disciples, even though they were slow to understand at times! We can listen in on these amazing conversations and ask the Holy Spirit to let us too be part of the receiving audience.

So, I pray that this week you will hear Jesus speaking to you through these verses each day: that he would speak into your life and where you are right at this moment, and that you would not remain unchanged.

Calling and answering

'Come, follow me,' Jesus said, 'and I will send you out to fish for people.' (NIV)

Like all of Jesus' sayings, this single line of text is so rich with meaning. He is calling his disciples, yes, but he is also calling us today, right at this very moment. Perhaps this is the first time you are hearing this call. Perhaps you answered it a very long time ago but now he has a new area of ministry for you.

For the disciples, answering this call meant physically putting down their nets, or current career, and trusting in Jesus to provide for all of their needs. A big leap of faith! For us it can be the same, when we first decide to follow Jesus or when we follow him into a new area. We may have to give up something or put it second to him – our family, income, ambition. To do this, we need to have the same faith as the disciples. I have found this hard at times, but thankfully God is very patient and kind, and I have grown in confidence from looking back to the plans he has previously worked out for the best.

Although we can't see him calling as they did and then physically follow him, we can make sure we know him well by spending time in prayer and reading his word. This will give us the assurance we need. He will never contradict his word in the Bible, so checking against that is a very good way to discern if something is really what God is saying to us, as is praying and discussing with other mature Christians.

We know that whatever the details, his call will still have the same ultimate goal as in the verse above – to fish for people – to spread the good news of the gospel to others.

Pray now that you would hear God calling you to follow him today and that he would give you the faith to go wherever he leads and be whatever he wants you to be.

KARIN LING

Faith and healing

Jesus said to him, 'I will go and heal him.' (NIV 1984)

In today's passage, Jesus uses this man's faith as an example and opportunity to teach his contemporaries, and we can still learn from it today. He shows that the gift and practice of faith can be found in anyone – in this unpopular soldier of the occupying Roman forces, or in ordinary me and you – and Jesus will respond to it. Interestingly Jesus response in verse 7 is translated differently in later versions of the NIV to imply that Jesus is asking a question as to whether he *should* come and heal him. However, I don't think that is the central point and indeed the account in Luke is quite different and doesn't quote Jesus' response directly at all. It just says that he goes! He responds to the faith.

In the next chapter of Matthew, Jesus speaks twice of faith when healing (in verses 22 and 29) as he does in many other episodes. There is a link.

It can be hard to have faith in very testing times such as sickness of a loved one. I have found this myself, with two of my four children suffering from chronic conditions. It gets hard to keep faith when praying daily and seeing no healing. However, Jesus says later in Matthew 17:20 that we only need faith as small as a mustard seed and we can move a mountain! If we pray and ask God to help us with our faith by his Holy Spirit, he will. We can also ask our Christian friends to pray for our faith in times it is understandably weakened. We must remember too that not all healing will happen in our time and on this earth, so the faith we need to have is also for the new creation that is coming. As it says in Revelation 21:4, all *will* be healed. Hallelujah!

Pray now for God to increase your faith, in order to keep praying for those you know who need his healing touch. Encourage the faith of other Christians you know are experiencing testing times.

KARIN LING

Hiding and revealing

At that time Jesus said, 'I praise you, Father, Lord of heaven and earth, because you have hidden these things from the wise and learned, and revealed them to little children.' (NIV)

How encouraging! If we ever worry that we are not wise and learned enough, we can take heart! Jesus gives respect to those who some would think unable of having 'strong' faith because of young age, lack of education or learning difficulties of some kind.

The 'wise and learned' at that time were the Pharisees or teachers of the biblical law, who had got themselves so tied up in following each rule, and judging those who did not, that they could no longer see the central teachings of the faith. They also couldn't see Jesus for who he was – the Son of God. As Jesus goes on to say in verse 27, by not knowing Jesus fully, they could not know God

Children accept things with such joy, wonder and excitement. When you see an adult come to faith for the first time, it is often the same. I know I felt such excitement after going on an Alpha course and being baptised. I couldn't stop talking about Jesus to anyone and everyone! I also found the new faith of a young woman in my Bible study group so refreshing. She had no Christian family background, as most of us did, and she prayed so differently and naturally. I learnt a lot from her – a child in terms of her faith.

As we get more mature as Christians, it may give us great wisdom, but we must ensure we don't lose our first child-like enthusiasm and love or become cynical and judgemental like the Pharisees. We too can become blinded to what Jesus is saying. We need to be open to learning from those who are different or younger in age and/or faith than us.

Lord, refresh us now. Make our love for you like that of a child filled with wonder and awe at all you have done for us. Help us to respect and learn from all those around us who follow you.

KARIN LING

Repeating and repeating!

'Be careful,' Jesus said to them. 'Be on your guard against the yeast of the Pharisees and Sadducees.' (NIV)

With four children and a husband, I get frustrated at having to say things more than once! It's comforting to hear Jesus in this passage, patiently going over things again until, at last, the disciples understand. I need to learn from this and also be encouraged: I need not be afraid to ask Jesus to make himself clearer to me.

In the verse above, Jesus is in fact warning against the false teaching of the rulers of the law at that time. They did not recognise Jesus as the Son of God but also changed the rules of the Old Testament laws to suit themselves. By using the analogy of yeast, Jesus is saying that it only takes a very small amount of this sort of lie to have a big effect on our lives, just as a pinch of yeast causes dough to swell up and change its very structure.

In our society, it is also widely accepted that a mixture of beliefs is okay and there is no single truth in life. However, in John 14:6, Jesus says the opposite – he is the only truth and the only way to God. We, too, need to be on our guard against any teaching or views that are not in line with the Bible – a yardstick with which we can measure the truth of anything we hear or read. We can ask God for a spirit of discernment so that we can feel instinctively if something is not of him. We can choose wise, godly mentors to be accountable to and ask advice from. Then we can keep any lies from working through into our lives to change us like that yeast in the dough.

Thank you, Jesus, that your teaching works in us to create the best and that is all we need. Help us to have wisdom and discernment to listen only to your truth.

KARIN LING

Losing and gaining

Then Jesus said to his disciples, 'Whoever wants to be my disciple must deny themselves and take up their cross and follow me.' (NIV)

In this passage, Jesus is talking about how he will soon give up his life for others, including you and me. To Peter and to most of us, this sounds terrible – death is something to be feared and avoided at all costs. However, Jesus firmly rebukes Peter for not seeing the necessity and significance of his sacrifice. He goes on to explain in the verse above that if we want to follow Jesus, we, too, need to be prepared to give up everything – including our very lives. Thankfully, for most of us, this will not involve physical death for being a Christian, but we know for many around the world that is the difficult truth. As Christians are starting to face more opposition here in the west, we can perhaps empathise better.

For us, it may be that we have to give up a job we no longer see is ethical or stop socialising with friends who indulge in gossip, drunkenness or drugs. Family members may decide to ostracise us for our new beliefs. There is real loss that can cause us true grief.

So why would we go through all this? In verse 25, Jesus tells us that by losing our lives for his sake we will indeed find them – true purpose and meaning which every human is searching for. We can see the truth of verse 26 lived out in the lives of many of those who achieve the fame or wealth which the world tells us we need to be happy and fulfilled: the 'successful' can often end up suffering from addictions, failed relationships, depression and even suicide. Only God can give us true satisfaction and peace – so that even when we are tested, we can take heart.

Jesus said: 'I have told you these things, so that in me you may have peace. In this world you will have trouble. But take heart! I have overcome the world' (John 16:33).

KARIN LING

Rebuking and accepting

Jesus said, 'Let the little children come to me, and do not hinder them, for the kingdom of heaven belongs to such as these.' (NIV)

Children are part of all our lives – whether we are parents, godparents, teachers, Sunday school leaders or just part of the church family, we all have a relationship to children. They can bring us great joy but also huge frustration! Children can be fun and refreshing but also demanding and difficult. It is particularly hard to get anything done with them around. We may have a day planned at home, a session at Sunday school or for a visiting family, and they completely go their own way!

In our passage today, we see Jesus as he is speaking and healing in the region of Judea. Large crowds had followed him and the Pharisees had come to test him. So when lots of kids turn up with runny noses, loud voices and sticky hands, he could be excused for finding it just too much. Also, at that time the very idea of using precious hours to minister specifically to children would have been considered silly. This is why the disciples rebuke the adults for wasting Jesus' time and throwing him off schedule.

However, in the verse above we see Jesus welcoming this distraction. As we saw in Matthew 11, Jesus is pointing out that children are important to God and that we have a lot to learn from them.

Romans 8:15–16 teaches that we adults are seen by God as his children; too often we go off track and frustrate his plans for us. As he was with the children in our passage, he always accepts us with open arms, ready to take time to bless us and show us the way forward.

I am still reeling from a very testing morning with one of my children, so pray with me now for renewed energy and patience as we care for the children in our lives. Lord, help us always make time to pray with them.

KARIN LING

Keeping hold and letting go

Then Jesus said to his disciples, 'Truly I tell you, it is hard for someone who is rich to enter the kingdom of heaven.' (NIV)

My first thought when I read this passage was that Jesus' words don't apply to me as I am not rich like the young man he is speaking to… but then I thought again. Compared to a lot of the world, if we have a roof over our heads and food on the table we are indeed rich. I also don't think of myself as materialistic and try to be generous… but then I think again. How attached am I to my creature comforts, and would I be prepared to give away so much that life became much harder for me? If any of us heard Jesus say this to us, how would we truthfully respond, face-to-face with him?

Just as importantly, what would the attitude of our hearts and minds be, even if our hands did give away some of our wealth? 2 Corinthians 9:7 says God loves a cheerful giver and our attitude needs to be right.

Do I recognise that all I have comes from God, and do I want whatever wealth I have to be used in line with his teaching?

It can feel confusing as to how much and how often and with whom we share. I have never found a better structure than that given in Leviticus 27:30, which says that a tenth (or tithe) of all we own should be given to God. It can be good practice to set up a direct debit to the various recipients so the amount comes out of the bank at the start of the month. Remember we are also called to be generous with the 90% remaining! Pray daily for guidance as to where God wants you to give and who to encourage with your money. And don't forget, we can't out-give God!

Lord, thank you for all you have given us and most importantly the promise of eternal life with you. Help us to be generous and give joyfully and graciously.
                                                                    KARIN LING

The Christmas story – and beyond

Claire Musters writes:

Advent means 'coming' – not just the celebration of the first Advent but a looking forward to our Saviour's second coming. Now is a time to slow down and consider afresh: do we live our lives in the light of the gospel message and our everlasting hope or do we get swallowed up by the mundane? We are gearing up towards Christmas, and you, like me, are probably rushing around getting final arrangements ready. My prayer for our time together is that these notes help you to slow down, press the pause button and embrace the time of waiting, of preparation, of looking forward – and remembering back, too, as we get closer to the end of the year.

When we look at the Christmas story through fresh eyes, we can home in on details that perhaps we have missed before. That is partly why I've focused (to begin with) on Luke's account: he includes so much detail he doesn't want us to miss.

As I reread this very familiar story, I was struck again by the gentle faith and obedience of Mary, particularly as her own journey got harder and harder. She responded to the angel Gabriel's message by acknowledging, 'I am the Lord's servant' (Luke 1:38, NIV), and that servant attitude is one that Jesus shared with her – and wants us to share as well. I was fascinated by how much Jesus' and John's stories intertwined, even before their moments of conception.

On one day we will be looking at the journey to Bethlehem, and Advent can remind us that we are all on a journey in our walk of faith with God. We will face frustrations, disappointment, fear as well as delight and celebration, just as those connected to the Christmas story did in their everyday lives. It can be heartening to know that we are not alone.

And what about beyond Christmas? Both Jesus and John the Baptist grew up to become proclaimers of God's truth – we will look at their first adult interaction recorded (at Jesus' baptism) as the year draws to a close, and we then look forward to a new year, which brings us closer to when our Saviour will return again. What should our priorities be as that fresh new year opens up before us?

Faithful in the waiting

Both of them [Zechariah and Elizabeth] were righteous in the sight of God, observing all the Lord's commands and decrees blamelessly. But they were childless because Elizabeth was not able to conceive, and they were both very old. (NIV)

We are not very good at waiting, are we? In an age of instant communication and so much available to purchase at the click of a button, we simply don't have to wait too frequently. And yet it is in the waiting that God often does his deepest work. This means we can find ourselves waiting for him to act. The wait may directly affect some of our deepest longings, and we can find that hard to bear. When you are asked to wait, what do you do with that time?

Elizabeth must have felt huge disappointment. For years she didn't have a choice but to wait patiently for the one thing in her culture that revealed God's blessing on a couple: children. She would have been faced with the shame of remaining childless. She was probably at the point of giving up, as both she and Zechariah were advanced in years.

We all have times when we feel we have done everything right, so surely God should give us the desires of our hearts. The passage tells us that Elizabeth was married to a priest and she herself 'was a descent of Aaron'. So she came from a ministry family, and we are told she was holy and righteous. There must have been tongues wagging, wondering what secret sin could possibly have caused her misfortune. In verse 25, Elizabeth provides insight into what she must have endured – 'disgrace among the people'.

We are not told how many years Elizabeth and Zechariah had to wait, but the text infers it was a long time. But when God's messenger arrived, at his appointed time rather than theirs, he was very specific about the child that would be born to them – and the instructions for them too.

Their age and Elizabeth's barrenness spoke louder to Zechariah than God's angel – so he was struck dumb. How often do you allow what you can see in front of you to cause you to doubt God, rather than waiting patiently?

CLAIRE MUSTERS

An unexpected visitor

'I am the Lord's servant,' Mary answered. 'May your word to me be fulfilled.' (NIV)

Gabriel is busy in this chapter! Not only was he the unexpected visitor to Zechariah, six months later he appeared to Mary, again with a message about a child that would be born and who would change the world.

Just imagine for a minute what this second visit must have been like for Mary. She was a young woman (probably still a teenager) and had recently got engaged to the carpenter Joseph. Her life seemed mapped out in front of her. And then Gabriel suddenly appeared to turn it upside down. Has God ever done that in your own life? I remember times when God has seemed to make a clear way forward and then, just a few short months later, closed the door. It can be confusing and difficult to deal with.

Mary, understandably, was perplexed by the sudden appearance of the angel and even more so by his message. She showed courage in being able to speak to him and ask him a direct question – I'm not sure I'd have stayed long enough for conversation! But when she heard the answer to how the baby Jesus would be conceived, she revealed her deep trust in God by simply affirming her standing as his servant and accepting the mission that she had been handpicked for.

Mary must have known the shame that she would have to endure in the coming months. There must have been a million questions flying through her mind, such as whether her fiancé would still be there after he heard her news. God sometimes asks us to do some unusual things, which can cause difficulties with those around us. But God views such times as opportunities to reveal his glory – as well as building our character.

God saw something in Mary that caused him to ask her to say yes to this unusual but vital task. If you are willing, he will use you for his purposes too. Why not say 'yes' to trusting him today?

CLAIRE MUSTERS

Pregnant pause

'As soon as the sound of your greeting reached my ears, the baby in my womb leaped for joy. Blessed is she who has believed that the Lord would fulfil his promises to her!' (NIV)

Gabriel had told Mary that Elizabeth was also pregnant, and so she took some time out to visit her relative. We can only speculate as to whether she left straight away, hearing Elizabeth's news and wanting to get away from any gossip or repercussions once her own news got out. What was wonderful was the welcome that she got from both Elizabeth and her unborn baby. God prepared the way: as the text tells us, Elizabeth was filled with the Holy Spirit and recognised that Mary was carrying the Messiah before she even said anything! What an encouragement for Mary, and she responded with a song of worship, declaring truths about the majesty of God and the faithfulness of his promises.

Both women were probably feeling the weight of expectations, each carrying a child that had been announced by God's messenger and declared as uniquely called for his purposes. By taking time out to come alongside one another, they were able to encourage each other – which we see happened straight away.

This encounter reminds me of how much I need those close female friends who encourage and champion the giftings God has placed inside of me.

I am struck by Elizabeth's response as the Holy Spirit touched her. She had waited so, so long for a child, and God had answered her prayer with an incredible promise that her son would be set apart to draw people back to God. And yet within six months her much younger, still unmarried relative arrived, pregnant with a child that was actually the Son of God! She could have been envious, but instead was overjoyed. Are we that gracious when a friend of ours is seemingly being blessed more than us?

Think about the female friends in your life. How can you encourage them today? Thank God for them and ask him to give you creative ways to show them how grateful you are that they are in your life.

CLAIRE MUSTERS

John's birth

'And you, my child, will be called a prophet of the Most High; for you will go on before the Lord to prepare the way for him.' (NIV)

The moment of John's arrival brought joy to the community that Elizabeth and Zechariah were a part of. But it also revealed how both parents had remained faithful to God and the message that Gabriel had brought. They kept to the Jewish customs and prepared to circumcise their baby on the eighth day. Those around them assumed they would carry on Zechariah's name, but Elizabeth courageously spoke up to say that he was to be called John. As soon as Zechariah backed her up in this, his tongue was loosened.

I see a picture of a unified couple here, as well as overjoyed and prayerful parents. Like Elizabeth before, Zechariah was filled with the Holy Spirit and prophesied, declaring praise (as Mary did in her song) about his faithful God. He talked of the way God had worked throughout history, before declaring the relationship that there would be between his son and Jesus.

Interestingly, there are parallels within his prophecy with Old Testament passages. For example, verses 69–71 uses imagery found in Psalm 132:17 ('I will make a horn grow for David'). The very words Zechariah spoke indicated that he was well versed in scripture. This is a great example to us to make sure we know our Bibles well!

It is amazing to think that God used a couple who had been barren for so many years to bring into the world a baby who would eventually prepare the way for Jesus. Don't underestimate what God can do through you – and, if you are a parent, through your children. And don't underestimate the power of praying for your children/other younger relatives and friends too.

Lord, I thank you for the birth of John and its importance in our Lord's journey. Help me to see how my life fits into the purposes you have for me and those around me.

CLAIRE MUSTERS

The journey

So Joseph also went up from the town of Nazareth in Galilee to Judea, to Bethlehem the town of David, because he belonged to the house and line of David. (NIV)

Luke was a doctor who was fastidious about including details other gospel writers didn't. He provides the explanation as to why Jesus was born in Bethlehem rather than Nazareth. The Roman census meant that everyone, regardless of age and status, had to travel back to their town of origin. God used even the corrupt Roman rule to fulfil Old Testament prophecy. (For example, Micah 5:2 foretold that the Messiah would come out of Bethlehem.) If he could do that, how much more should we believe him able to work in our own daily circumstances?

Mary and Joseph's journey would have been arduous. The distance was around 90 miles, foot and donkey were the means and they would have had to carry enough provisions to last. They would have camped out in whatever terrain they found themselves in – imagine doing that heavily pregnant! The last part of their journey would have been the hardest, as Bethlehem is situated on a hill. At this point, they must have been exhausted and anxious, as Mary was close to delivery.

We can dismiss situations as not being of God when we hit obstacles, and yet here we see the mother and adoptive father of our Messiah forcing themselves to put one foot in front of another just to reach Bethlehem – then on arrival there was nowhere comfortable to stay! How quickly do we get disappointed if circumstances make us uncomfortable? But God's highest priority is not our comfort.

The Roman rulers were viewed as gods; what a contrast to Jesus the baby! His entry into the world was lowly but was a sign of things to come. Jesus himself said, 'The Son of Man did not come to be served, but to serve, and to give his life as a ransom for many' (Matthew 20:28).

Lord, I cannot begin to imagine how difficult and uncomfortable the reality of travelling and giving birth would have been for Mary. I am sorry that I can grumble when circumstances get tough. Help me to persevere today.

CLAIRE MUSTERS

Good news of great joy!

An angel of the Lord appeared to [the shepherds], and the glory of the Lord shone around them, and they were terrified. But the angel said to them, 'Do not be afraid. I bring you good news that will cause great joy for all the people.' (NIV)

Happy Christmas!

I know that our traditional nativities always include the wise men, but I am encouraged by the fact that the first people to hear about Jesus' birth were lowly shepherds. Situated in the nearby fields, it is to them that the angel brought the 'good news'. This encounter speaks to me of the roles that Jesus would undertake: he called himself the good shepherd in John 10:14–15: 'I am the good shepherd; I know my sheep and my sheep know me – just as the Father knows me and I know the Father – and I lay down my life for the sheep.' He points to the sacrificial role he would have as the lamb of God. In his own gospel, John describes Jesus using this very same term: 'The next day John saw Jesus coming towards him and said, "Look, the Lamb of God, who takes away the sin of the world!"' (John 1:29).

Having experienced the glory of God, the shepherds hurry to see the child, but afterwards they don't keep the good news to themselves; they were obviously convincing in their retelling, as verse 18 indicates that 'all who heard it were amazed'.

I know from my own experience that speaking up about the good news is something I can find quite difficult, so this passage is certainly a challenge to me. But I believe that it doesn't matter how eloquent we are, as it is the Holy Spirit who works in hearts and minds (as we've already seen). People are often more interested in 'reading' our lives, so are we consistent in the way we live? The shepherds, we are told, continued to glorify and praise God once back in the fields.

Coping with the journey and then giving birth would have left her exhausted; then the shepherds arrived, but Mary quietly 'treasured' it all in her heart. In the business of Christmas Day, may we take time to do the same.

CLAIRE MUSTERS

Recognising the Messiah

'My eyes have seen your salvation, which you have prepared in the sight of all nations: a light for revelation to the Gentiles, and the glory of your people Israel.' (NIV)

Joseph and Mary followed Jewish law, so they took Jesus to be purified and presented at the temple. While there, they had two encounters with older, God-fearing people who spoke God's words over their child (even words that foretold the pain Jesus' calling held for Mary – see verse 35). Simeon was hanging on to a promise from God that he would see the Messiah before dying and, again through the Holy Spirit's revelation, recognised Jesus for who he was. Anna had remained faithful to God even after the bitter pain of early widowhood and was recognised in the temple as a prophetess. Both these people, like Elizabeth and Zechariah, are great examples of patient waiting. When Jesus arrived, they immediately recognised that salvation would be found in him. We are told in verse 38 that Anna continued to tell people about Jesus.

Too often we can dismiss the words of older people (I know I did when I was younger), but in their society age would have held weight. Today our society holds up the ideals of youth, fitness and beauty, but let's learn from these two that remaining close to God is the most important thing – and that he can speak through us whatever our age.

I love how actively involved both Simeon and Anna were in the temple, and it reminds me that God brings purpose to our lives whatever season we may find ourselves in. I struggled with that when I had young children, but it was when an older woman in our church asked me whether I played worship music in our home that I suddenly realised that I had stopped doing so. As I began to play it again, and worship was stirred in my soul once more, I began to experience joy afresh.

Lord, I refuse to buy into the myth that it is only the young and outwardly beautiful who are of use. Help me to recognise how you would like me to minister to those around me today – younger and older.

CLAIRE MUSTERS

In his Father's house

'Why were you searching for me?' [Jesus] asked. 'Didn't you know I had to be in my Father's house?' But they did not understand what he was saying to them. (NIV)

At the age of twelve, Jesus would have been considered almost an adult, so it was not unusual for someone his age to be fairly independent from his family. Still, we can read this passage and wonder how his parents could have travelled for a full day without realising Jesus wasn't with them! But to provide protection for one another against bandits, people often travelled in groups, with the women and children all together and the men behind. So mother and father could each have assumed that Jesus was with the other (as he was at that age in Jewish culture that straddled both childhood and adulthood). Little did they know that he had already found his place and was astounding those around him with his knowledge and insight.

Mary showed the love and care of a mother when she challenged Jesus, revealing their close relationship. But his answer must have cut deep. It reminds me of when Jesus bluntly pointed out that following him would call for sacrifice – and might upset those around us. See how strongly he puts it in Matthew 10:37–38: 'Anyone who loves their father or mother more than me is not worthy of me... Whoever does not take up their cross and follow me is not worthy of me.'

While Jesus had to follow his heavenly Father over and above his earthly parents, this does not mean he dishonoured them. Remember how, on the cross, he thought of his mother and best friend, asking them to look after each other (John 19:26).

There is mention again of how his mother treasured up all that she experienced, even though she was beginning to understand how his calling would hurt her – what a challenge to us!

Take some time to prayerfully consider whether you have allowed anyone or anything to take the place of Jesus in your life. Allow the Holy Spirit to lead you in repentance.

CLAIRE MUSTERS

Preparing the way

A voice of one calling in the wilderness, 'Prepare the way for the Lord, make straight paths for him. Every valley shall be filled in, every mountain and hill made low. The crooked roads shall become straight, the rough ways smooth. And all people will see God's salvation.' (NIV)

Luke starts by explaining exactly when it was that John received the message he was to proclaim. This was John's time to fulfil the calling that had been spoken over him before conception and at the time of his circumcision – to prepare the way for Jesus.

Like many Old Testament prophets before him, John stood out as an unusual character. The parallel verses in Matthew 3:1–12 tell us that he wore camel's hair and ate locusts, while living out in the wilderness. And yet there was something magnetic about his proclamations, and so people travelled to hear him regardless of his appearance, even wondering if he was the Messiah.

John was very clear in his identity and was at pains to point out that he was not worthy in comparison to the one he was announcing. I don't think this was false humility or a sense of low self-worth, as we might interpret it. He was confident in what he was called to do (to share the good news of the one coming and to baptise people as a sign of repentance), while recognising and honouring the supreme worth of Jesus.

I know that identity is an issue that we can struggle with as women – as is knowing a clear sense of calling. They are both things I have found difficult over the years. We are bombarded with messages from culture about what we should look like and what we should be able to achieve. And yet, taking time to slow down and listen to what Jesus says about us is so vital if we are going to live our lives confident in the knowledge that we are accepted, called and chosen by him. Then we can truly reflect the good news as we go about our everyday business.

Take some time out to simply ask Jesus what he wants to remind you about your identity today. Thank him that because of his worthiness, you are worthy before God too.

CLAIRE MUSTERS

Crossed paths

Jesus replied, 'Let it be so now; it is proper for us to do this to fulfil all righteousness.' Then John consented. (NIV)

This is the moment when these two men, whose lives had been purposed by God to be interconnected, finally met as adults (they may well have met as children, as their mothers were relatives).

I have chosen the Matthew account because there is an important detail I'd like to focus on. Verse 14 tells us that, when faced with Jesus coming to be baptised, John had a wobble. He knew that Jesus was the Messiah, so it appears he had a moment when he felt unqualified – and told Jesus so. But look at Jesus' response: he immediately reminds him that God had preordained this moment.

Jesus had not sinned, but was identifying with those who had been humble enough to repent, as well as marking the start of his public ministry. And how beautifully his Father and the Holy Spirit endorsed what he was doing!

I know that there are times when I am about to step out and do what God has asked me to do, but then I get overwhelmed, feeling I simply can't. In those moments I have learned to remind myself that I should not be trying to do things in my own strength; rather, I can and should lean on God. Sometimes I need those around me to do the reminding; I love how God brings people into our lives for particular purposes at particular times.

John still had to step out and do what was asked of him, and that included not only speaking about the Messiah but being willing to submit to him (and point his own followers to Jesus). When things are going well, do we acknowledge God's hand? And if God asks us to relinquish our hold on them, are we quick to do so or do we struggle?

Lord, it is beautiful to read about how John submitted to and baptised you, and how your Father spoke words of affirmation over you. Help me to put my own ego aside to encourage others to draw closer to you.

CLAIRE MUSTERS

Having a servant heart

'Whoever wants to become great among you must be your servant, and whoever wants to be first must be your slave.' (NIV)

Back on 24 December, we touched on the fact that Jesus said he came to serve rather than be served. However, I think this is such an important part of his teaching – and something that we can find so difficult – that I want to spend today looking at it more closely.

We can read this story of James and John wanting the best seats in heaven and look down on them, and yet we are not so different. As Jesus pointed out to the disciples who got indignant, we can all wish for recognition, yet true discipleship calls for a willingness to serve and prefer one another.

Those of us who are mothers may also painfully recognise a tendency to want to push our own children forwards, to ensure they get the best of every opportunity. Are we able to trust that God's will for their lives is the most important – and right – path for them to take, wherever that may lead?

The cup that Jesus refers to in verse 22 is suffering. I am challenged each time a baby is dedicated at our church, as there is a line that asks the new parents, 'If God calls your child to a life of great sacrifice, do you promise to neither complain nor try to hold them back?' The truth is, we are called to share in his sufferings, not for suffering's sake, but in order to share his glory (see Romans 8:17).

When Jesus prayed for his disciples, and specifically for us too, in John 17, he indicated that it would be through our unity that the world would know him. We cannot be in true unity without laying down our lives – including our own personal preferences. What a sobering call to honestly appraise our motivations today.

Lord, if I am being truly honest, I can find being a servant difficult. Sometimes everything in me wants to push myself forwards, rather than laying down my life for others. Help me to follow your example today.

                                                                    CLAIRE MUSTERS

Submitting our lives afresh

He died for all, that those who live should no longer live for themselves but for him who died for them and was raised again. (NIV)

Each time a year draws to a close, I take time to think back over the past year (the highs and lows, what I learned and what I struggled with) and look forward to the new year and the things I feel God is stirring in me.

I love this passage, because it contains so much truth we can take into the new year. We do groan, because we are living with the tension of looking forward to our eternal home but still remaining here on earth. We are burdened at times, because we face difficulties and trials. We need to remember that Jesus told us that we will have trouble in this world but can know peace because he has overcome (John 16:33). He has also given us the Holy Spirit as a deposit of what is to come, and as our guide and comforter now.

We are reminded in verse 16 that we are no longer to live for ourselves – what a great reminder at the turn of the year! Rather than feeling condemned by this, we should rejoice that we are new creations who can live by faith! God has not only saved us but has given us roles as his ambassadors to this world.

We have seen how the births of Jesus and John were foretold, and how they fulfilled their God-given destinies. As these notes draw to a close, may we settle our hearts to submit afresh to God, and to live each day in the will of God by asking what he would have us do. I have found two simple prayers so helpful in my daily life: 'Lord, please order my day' and 'What is the one thing you want me to do today, Lord?' I hope they will help you too.

Lord, I thank you for the way that you have held me through this year. Help me to remember all that you have taught me and to live for you alone in the coming year.

CLAIRE MUSTERS

Were you there? BRF celebrates its centenary in 2022 and we'd love you to share your BRF memories with us. We've already heard from supporters with wonderful stories. Beryl Fudge attended our 25th anniversary service in Westminster Central Hall in 1947, in the presence of the Queen Mother and Princess Margaret. Catharine Heron was prepared for confirmation in 1945 by our founder, Canon Leslie Mannering, and still has his duplicated notes in their original brown cardboard folder.

Do you have a BRF story to tell, whether of events, people, books or Bible reading notes? Please email **eley.mcainsh@brf.org.uk**, call **01865 319708** or write to **Eley McAinsh** at BRF, 15 The Chambers, Vineyard, Abingdon, OX14 3FE, United Kingdom.

Recommended reading

A Better Song to Sing
Finding life again through the invitations of Jesus
Mags Duggan
978 0 85746 876 5 £8.99
brfonline.org.uk

Many sincere followers of Jesus are secretly disappointed, dissatisfied and quietly desperate for more than they are currently experiencing. That *more* is found as we respond to the invitations of Jesus, which hold out to us the hope of dynamic change, of a truly vibrant, transformed life – a better song to sing. Each chapter explores one specific invitation, drawing out its possible implications for our lives, and suggests a spiritual practice or reflection to help us ground that invitation in our present-day reality.

The Bible Doesn't Tell Me So
Why you don't have to submit to domestic abuse and coercive control
Helen Paynter
978 0 85746 989 2 £8.99
brfonline.org.uk

This book is addressed directly to women experiencing domestic abuse. It aims to debunk the myths – propagated perhaps intentionally by some abusers, and unwittingly by many churches – which prevent women from getting out of harm's way. It aims to help them come to see that the Bible does not belong to their abuser, but that it is a text of liberation. Written with careful attention to pastoral issues, it closely but accessibly examines and explains the relevant scriptural texts.

To order

Online: **brfonline.org.uk**
Telephone: +44 (0)1865 319700
Mon–Fri 9.15–17.30

Delivery times within the UK are normally 15 working days. Prices are correct at the time of going to press but may change without prior notice.

Title	Price	Qty	Total
A Better Song to Sing	£8.99		
The Bible Doesn't Tell Me So	£8.99		
Day by Day with God (Jan–Apr 2021) – single copy	£4.70		
Day by Day with God (May–Aug 2021) – single copy	£4.70		

POSTAGE AND PACKING CHARGES			
Order value	UK	Europe	Rest of world
Under £7.00	£2.00		
£7.00–£29.99	£3.00	Available on request	Available on request
£30.00 and over	FREE		

Total value of books	
Postage and packing	
Total for this order	

Please complete in BLOCK CAPITALS

Title _____ First name/initials _____ Surname _____

Address _____

_____ Postcode _____

Acc. No. _____ Telephone _____

Email _____

Method of payment

❏ Cheque (made payable to BRF) ❏ MasterCard / Visa credit / Visa debit

Card no. ☐☐☐☐ ☐☐☐☐ ☐☐☐☐ ☐☐☐☐ ☐☐☐☐

Expires end ☐☐ ☐☐   Security code* ☐☐☐   Last 3 digits on the reverse of the card

Signature* _____ Date _____ / _____ / _____

*ESSENTIAL IN ORDER TO PROCESS YOUR ORDER

Please return this form to:
BRF, 15 The Chambers, Vineyard, Abingdon OX14 3FE | **enquiries@brf.org.uk**
To read our terms and find out about cancelling your order, please visit **brfonline.org.uk/terms.**

The Bible Reading Fellowship (BRF) is a Registered Charity (233280)

SUBSCRIPTION INFORMATION

Each issue of *Day by Day with God* is available from Christian bookshops everywhere. Copies may also be available through your church book agent or from the person who distributes Bible reading notes in your church.

Alternatively you may obtain *Day by Day with God* on subscription direct from the publishers. There are two kinds of subscription:

Individual subscriptions
covering 3 issues for 4 copies or less, payable in advance
(including postage & packing).

To order, please complete the details on page 144 and return with the appropriate payment to: BRF, 15 The Chambers, Vineyard, Abingdon OX14 3FE

You can also use the form on page 144 to order a gift subscription for a friend.

Group subscriptions
covering 3 issues for 5 copies or more, sent to one UK address (post free).

Please note that the annual billing period for group subscriptions runs from 1 May to 30 April.

To order, please complete the details on page 143 and return with the appropriate payment to: BRF, 15 The Chambers, Vineyard, Abingdon OX14 3FE

You will receive an invoice with the first issue of notes.

All our Bible reading notes can be ordered online by visiting
brfonline.org.uk/collections/subscriptions

Day by Day with God is also available as
an app for Android, iPhone and iPad
brfonline.org.uk/collections/apps

Follow us on Instagram: **@daybydaywithgod**

All subscription enquiries should be directed to:
BRF, 15 The Chambers, Vineyard, Abingdon OX14 3FE
+44 (0)1865 319700 | **enquiries@brf.org.uk**

DAY BY DAY WITH GOD GROUP SUBSCRIPTION FORM

All our Bible reading notes can be ordered online by visiting
brfonline.org.uk/collections/subscriptions

The group subscription rate for *Day by Day with God* will be £14.10 per person
until April 2021.

☐ I would like to take out a group subscription for _____ (quantity) copies.

☐ Please start my order with the January 2021 / May 2021 / September 2021*
issue. (*delete as appropriate)

Please do not send any money with your order. Send your order to BRF and we
will send you an invoice.

Name and address of the person organising the group subscription:

Title _____ First name/initials _____ Surname _____

Address_____

_____ Postcode _____

Telephone _____ Email _____

Church_____

**Name and address of the person paying the invoice if the invoice needs to be
sent directly to them:**

Title _____ First name/initials _____ Surname _____

Address_____

_____ Postcode _____

Telephone _____ Email _____

Please return this form to:
BRF, 15 The Chambers, Vineyard, Abingdon OX14 3FE | **enquiries@brf.org.uk**

To read our terms and find out about cancelling your order,
please visit **brfonline.org.uk/terms**.

To order online, please visit **brfonline.org.uk/collections/subscriptions**

☐ I would like to give a gift subscription (please provide both names and addresses)
☐ I would like to take out a subscription myself (complete your name and address details only once)

Title .... First name/initials .... Surname ....

Address ....

.... Postcode ....

Telephone .... Email ....

Gift subscription name ....

Gift subscription address ....

.... Postcode ....

Gift subscription (20 words max. or include your own gift card):

....

....

Please send *Day by Day with God* beginning with the January 2021 / May 2021 / September 2021 issue (*delete as appropriate*):

(*please tick box*)	UK	Europe	Rest of world
1-year subscription	☐ £17.85	☐ £25.80	☐ £29.70
2-year subscription	☐ £33.90	N/A	N/A

Total enclosed £ .... (cheques should be made payable to 'BRF')

Please charge my MasterCard / Visa credit / Visa debit with £ ....

Card no. ☐☐☐☐ ☐☐☐☐ ☐☐☐☐ ☐☐☐☐

Expires end ☐☐ ☐☐   Security code* ☐☐☐   Last 3 digits on the reverse of the card

Signature* .... Date ...... / ...... / ......
*ESSENTIAL IN ORDER TO PROCESS YOUR ORDER

Please return this form to:
BRF, 15 The Chambers, Vineyard, Abingdon OX14 3FE | enquiries@brf.org.uk

To read our terms and find out about cancelling your order, please visit **brfonline.org.uk/terms**. The Bible Reading Fellowship is a Registered Charity (233280)

DBDWG0320